The Guide to
Geopath
How Earth Energies Affect Your Life

Jane Thurnell-Read has spent over 20 years as a complementary therapist and teacher. She has written many articles and been interviewed on television and radio about her work. Her book *Health Kinesiology* was published in 2002.

The Guide to
Geopathic Stress
How Earth Energies Affect Your Life

Jane Thurnell-Read

First published by Element Books Ltd 1995
© Vega 2002
Text © Jane Thurnell-Read 1995

All rights reserved. No part of this book may be reproduced, stored in a retrieval system or transmitted in any form or by any means, electronic, mechanical, photocopying, recording or otherwise, without the prior permission in writing of the copyright owners.

ISBN 1 84333 529 8
A catalogue record for this book is available
from the British Library

Published in 2002 by Vega, 64 Brewery Road, London, N7 9NT
Visit our website at www.chrysalisbooks.co.uk

A member of Chrysalis Books plc

Jacket design: Grade Design Consultants
Managing Editor: Laurence Henderson
Production: Susan Sutterby

Printed and bound in Great Britain by
Creative Print and Design Wales

This book is dedicated
to my sons
Jonathan and Thomas

ACKNOWLEDGEMENTS

Many people have helped me formulate my ideas for this book, but I would particularly like to mention the following: Dr Jimmy Scott of Ontario, Canada, who has taught me so much about Health Kinesiology and geopathic stress; Dr Stephen Wright, who checked parts of the book for scientific accuracy; Irvin Klein for his help with some of the illustrations.

I would especially like to thank John Payne for his careful but gentle criticism of the manuscript. His insight and help were invaluable.

CONTENTS

Acknowledgements	vi
Introduction	ix
1 Geopathic Stress and its Symptoms	1
2 Geopathic Stress and Electromagnetism	14
3 Types of Geopathic Energy	26
4 How Geopathic Stress Affects the Body	36
5 The Subtle Energy System	48
6 Detecting Geopathic Stress	62
7 Correcting Geopathic Stress	76
8 Geopathic Stress and Feng Shui	91
9 Self-Help and Protection for the Individual	99
10 Looking Ahead	108
Appendix: Sick Building Syndrome	114
Notes	119
Bibliography	121
Useful Addresses	123
Index	128

INTRODUCTION

Have you ever walked into a building and found yourself feeling ill at ease? Maybe it felt cold or inhospitable, or perhaps there was something else that you could not quite put your finger on. In these places we may get shivers down our spine and feel uneasy. We look around trying to find what is wrong, trying to discover what is making us feel this way, but often there is nothing obvious. We try to reassure ourselves, but all we know is that we do not like the building and do not want to stay there any longer than necessary. Usually we leave as soon as possible without being able to explain our reservations about the place. What we may have experienced in these situations is a subconscious response to geopathic stress.

Geopathic comes from two Greek words: *geo* meaning 'of the earth', and *pathos*, meaning 'suffering' or 'disease'. The word geopathic literally means suffering or disease of the earth, so geopathic stress is the general term for energies emanating from the earth that can cause discomfort and ill health in human beings. Intuitive responses, such as those indicated above, may be warning us not to stay in such places, because of the damage long-term exposure can do to our bodies and minds.

When looking for a new home, we are unlikely to purchase a geopathically stressed house, even if it is exactly what we want in all other respects. A deep, instinctive feeling warns us of unpleasantness, perhaps even danger, and sometimes we heed this silent voice. However, some people dismiss these instinctive feelings because they cannot see any explanation for them. They would perhaps itemize everything they like about the house, set this against their inexplicable feelings and decide that the sensible and logical thing to do is to forget the latter and buy the house anyway. This is particularly likely if anyone else involved in the purchase does not have the same response. Some people do not seem to feel the warning signs or, if they do, are not conscious of them.

If exposure to geopathic energies is short lived, then in general the effects are insignificant, although some people will show symptoms of tiredness, inattention and headaches when sitting in a geopathically stressed area for even one or two hours. Inattentiveness in long meetings is not necessarily a sign of boredom. An engineer once challenged me to predict who would feel unwell during an afternoon spent in a particular lecture theatre. My prediction was to be based on the location of negative energy in the room. During his lecture he asked people to raise their hand if they had a headache or felt unwell in some way. Many of the people who responded were sitting in the seats I had designated. Even allowing for the fact that some people would have felt unwell anyway, the correlation was very strong. Any effect from short-term exposure like this will be transitory, with the body quickly recovering and returning to its normal state. Problems only occur when people spend a long time in places where the earth's energy is disturbed, perhaps when an individual's house or work place (or sometimes even both) is above an area of high geopathic stress.

As building land becomes increasingly scarce there is less and less choice about where houses are built. And if builders and architects had any understanding of geopathic stress, there would be even fewer options. As it is, the siting of buildings is determined on purely commercial grounds, taking into account land prices, proximity to transport and so on. The day when building sites are routinely assessed for geopathic stress is a long way off.

Nowadays people may live in the same building for many years and their exposure to a particular form of negative energy could last a long time. Rolf Gordon, the founder of the Dulwich

Health Society, has remarked that gypsies very rarely get cancer. Gordon believes this is because they move from place to place and any exposure to a 'bad' place would be for only a couple of weeks at most. He also notes that when choosing a site gypsies will take into account the feel of a place. There is no conclusive proof for Gordon's theory, but it is an interesting one. There is, however, some evidence that in more 'primitive' times, humans had some understanding of these matters and would build appropriately, taking into account the feel of the land.

Geopathic energy is an insidious phenomenon: we cannot see it or adequately explain it in current scientific terms, but the effects of it are likely to prove at least as devastating as environmental pollution. Geopathic energies pass through walls, windows and closed doors – they do not recognize boundaries, walls or fences. Geopathic energies are not fixed and stable – they may change according to the season or time of day. They may also change because of building work, even if it is being carried out in houses some way off, as geopathic energies can be distorted and transferred to buildings other than where work is taking place.

There are many different types of geopathic energies. Each one has a different effect on people, with some individuals being more susceptible than others. Sleeping, living or working consistently in a geopathically stressed area leads to emotional and physical problems and difficulties, which exact a heavy toll on both sufferers and their families. In today's frenetic world this is just one more stress that people may be exposed to, undermining their health and enthusiasm for life. Unfortunately, because so little is known about the subject, people do not realize what is happening. They are not aware that it is possible to make changes that can inactivate these negative earth energies and allow people to avoid serious ill health, or regain previous good health and well-being. Perhaps one day it will become commonplace to have a geopathic survey done on a new house or building site. If necessary, remedial action would then have to be taken by the owner or builder in order to ensure a sale. Similarly, it would hopefully become unthinkable to build a hospital on a site which had not been checked, or to make changes to the fabric of a school without looking at the energy implications.

Initial interest in the idea of geopathic stress was stimulated by the work of Winzer and Melzer in Germany in the 1920s. In Stuttgart they found that geological faults occurred in the areas of the city with the highest incidence of cancer. Gustav Freiherr von Pohl took this work further and studied two other places: Vilsbiburg, which had a very high incidence of cancer, and Grafenau, which had a very low incidence. In Vilsbiburg, von Pohl accurately predicted the incidence of cancer by dowsing for 'water veins' using a 1:1,000 scale map of the town. This survey was greeted with some scepticism as the town was small (8,300 inhabitants) and the cancer rate high. Von Pohl then turned his attention to Grafenau, the town with the lowest incidence of cancer in the area. Once again he was able to show a link between cancer cases and geopathic zones.[1]

Interest in geopathic stress has continued to the present day in Germany, and is also strong in France, where much of the other work in this field has been carried out. A large part of the research in these two countries has been associated with trying to identify the characteristics of geopathic phenomena. Other countries, perhaps due in part to scientific scepticism, have been more reluctant to investigate the subject. Clearly, our knowledge in this field is limited, but this does not mean these energies do not exist. Their existence is inferred from their effect on humans, animals and plants. In physics and biology too, much of our knowledge is, at least initially, inferred, with the existence of phenomena extrapolated from what can be seen and measured in the everyday world. Models can be produced to suggest that a certain thing must happen or be there because of the resulting activity, even though the process or phenomenon cannot itself be mapped. Sceptics seem to be particularly impressed with the fact that animals are also affected by geopathic energies, and it is hoped there will be more well-documented case studies in this area.

Although understanding of geopathic stress is still in its infancy, even our current knowledge and experience can make a dramatic difference to people's lives. Already it is possible to help many people who would otherwise suffer daily damage to their health and well-being. It is this possibility that has prompted me to write this book. There is very little material available on the subject and I felt it was important that more people should have access to the knowledge about these energies that disturb our environment. The main detection methods are fully explained and there is much practical advice on preventative and corrective measures. I have cited many case studies to show how these negative energies can be successfully corrected. Although often dismissed by scientists as anecdotal evidence, this does not mean these accounts are untrue or not worthy of consideration. As more and more information becomes available, the evidence becomes increasingly persuasive.

My own interest in geopathic stress came about as a result of inconsistencies I was finding in my natural healthcare practice. For many years now I have been helping people with a wide range of health problems using a healing system called Health Kinesiology. Although I have had many dramatic successes across a whole range of symptoms and illnesses, both physical and psychological, at one time some of my clients were unexpectedly not responding to treatment. I do not expect to be successful with everyone, but over the years I have developed an instinct for knowing the people I can help. And yet here was a small group of clients whose condition ought to have been improving, but for some reason was not. It would be easy to dismiss these people as hypochondriacs who did not want to get better, but it was very clear to me that many of them did not fall into this category. I began to wonder if geopathic stress was the missing link. When I started taking this into account, I found that many of these clients, often with seemingly intractable problems, started to get better.

I cannot say how these energies can be measured in a way that would satisfy the rigours of a scientific method, but I am certain that geopathic stress is a real phenomenon. This belief is based on my work with many clients and on seeing their response when their homes or work places were corrected for this strange and subtle energy. I have written about what I know from experience to be correct, and I hope readers will be able to benefit from my observations and increase their knowledge of the energies in their environment – and take steps to correct them if necessary.

1

Geopathic Stress and its Symptoms

Geopathic stress (GS) is the effect of negative earth energies ('negative' in this context meaning detrimental rather than having a negative electrical charge). Some people use the term geopathic stress only to describe ley lines (man-made energy lines) or energy disturbances caused by underground water. Yet others use the term in a way which includes both energy disturbances from the earth and man-made electromagnetic pollution such as power lines, radio waves, and so on. In this book we will be looking at the whole range of negative energies and their sources. People who restrict geopathic stress to either ley lines or underground water ignore many energies that have a destructive effect on people's health.

SOURCES OF GEOPATHIC ENERGY

The Earth's Magnetic Field

The earth has a natural magnetic field; it acts as though it has a large magnet at its centre. The rotation of the earth creates electric currents in the molten metals found within the earth's core, thereby producing a magnetic field. Human beings have evolved with this background magnetic field; they are accustomed to living in its presence. It is also thought that birds use the earth's magnetic field for migration purposes, and that whales may navigate great distances by monitoring it. This magnetic field is constantly changing by small amounts in various ways – which most people can cope with. Some natural variation in the earth's static magnetic field is brought about by changes in weather conditions – for instance, it increases during stormy weather – but this too does not appear to cause problems. People are also exposed to time-varying magnetic fields, mainly brought about by changes in the sun's activity, but again these do not seem to have a negative effect on people. *Geopathic stress occurs when the earth's magnetic field is disturbed, either naturally or artificially, and the background field we normally experience is changed.*

Natural Disturbances

Natural disturbances to the earth's magnetic field include geological faults, underground ore masses and underground water, particularly running water. These sorts of disturbances are relatively stable, although earthquakes and running underground water can slowly erode rock and have a destabilizing effect. Water is one of the few liquids that conducts electricity, which is why we have to be so careful with electricity in the bathroom. The potential for its inappropriate transmission is much higher because of the amount of water around, and the combination of water and electricity is a lethal one. It is perhaps for this reason that the original interest in geopathic stress very much focused on the effects of underground water. This type of disturbance has always been present, causing imbalances in the earth's energy field.

Rolf Gordon, the founder of the Dulwich Health Society, is quoted as saying:

> Natural radiations which rise up through the earth are distorted by weak electromagnetic fields created by subterranean running water, certain mineral concentrations, fault lines and under-

ground cavities. The wavelength of the natural radiation disturbed in this way becomes harmful to living organisms.[2]

Rodney Girdlestone, in an article entitled 'Are You Building In A Safe Place?' writes:

> Geopathic zones are characterized by variations in terrestrial magnetism, for the earth's field is not uniform but exhibits many highly localized distortions, some random, some fairly regular. They . . . occur over geological faults, caves and underground water-courses. These are places where the earth's natural and beneficial field increases or decreases rapidly (there is a high magnetic gradient). Flows of water underground produce the largest effects – and sewers and drains can be as big a hazard as underground streams.[3]

Jacob Stängle, a German engineer, developed a machine to test for gamma rays. Normally there is a background level of gamma radiation, but Stängle invented a machine – a scintillator – to test for variations in this level. He found that underground water veins showed a small increase in the levels of gamma rays at the surface. This increase correlated well with the depth and flow rate of the water.[4]

Man-Made Disturbances

Man-made disturbances to the earth's magnetic field include mining, foundations for tall buildings, underground transport systems and public utilities (sewage, water and so on). These disturbances are of more recent origin than natural ones, and have increased as man has made technological advances, changing his use of and relationship to the earth.

It will be interesting to see if the new Thames Water Ring Main surrounding London will influence earth energies in the area. The water from the treatment plant flows down a 40-metre drop into the Ring Main and is then taken out again at 11 main pump-out shafts throughout London. The pipes carry 285 million gallons of water to 6 million people every day. To monitor this, computers constantly check the quality and quantity of water along its 50-mile length. As well as flowing underground water there are sudden changes in water levels, both of which have been implicated in the production of geopathic stress.

In many areas mine workings can spread out for several miles beyond the pit head, and public utilities (such as sewage and water mains), while contributing in many ways to improving public health, may also be affecting earth energies and leading to a deterioration in public health. Foundations for tall buildings go very deep and again may affect geopathic energies.

It is, of course, possible that man-made structures and intervention improve a situation, by funnelling negative energies away from homes and other buildings. But I very rarely hear of such results because in such a situation people like me are not needed. Obviously, our concern is with a situation made worse by man's activities, because then something needs to be done. When things improve without explanation, this may be because of other building work nearby, but we soon tend to take these improvements for granted. These examples illustrate the fact that geopathic stress problems are continually changing in response to man's use of his environment. But as yet, people are just not sufficiently aware of the need to consider earth energies when siting a building, widening a road or digging a tunnel.

Both natural and man-made disturbances funnel and concentrate the earth's natural magnetic energy so that problems can be caused for not only humans but some animals and plants.

Other Sources

Geopathic stress has often been described as though it is always electromagnetic in origin. However, some of the damaging energies are almost certainly vibrating at a level beyond the electromagnetic spectrum currently detected and recognized by conventional science and technology. It is also possible that some of the energies are of a completely different nature and not electromagnetic at all.

Paul Schmidt in a booklet entitled *Earth Rays* (page 3) writes:

> Earth Rays are not uniform, but the combination of rays and different waves. Through my own observation I have discovered that the rays that can be measured on a Geiger counter are of little importance in this area. Waves are the crucial part of the energy between the cosmos and the earth. They form a regular energy field between the cosmos and the earth, which is concentrated over displacements, underground water sources, faults and cavities (caves), but also over ore deposits, in a similar way to the concentration of the sun's rays in a magnifying glass.

This describes a source of geopathic energies which is not primarily within the earth's magnetic field. It is unclear whether Schmidt is seeing the cosmic rays interacting with the earth's magnetic field, or as being separate from it.

To sum up, geopathic energies are detrimental energies mainly emanating from the earth and leading to long-term harm to susceptible humans who are exposed to them either in their place of work or at home.

EFFECTS OF GEOPATHIC STRESS

There are several different ways in which geopathic stress can affect people, whatever the source of the energy disturbance. And as the effect is insidious, it is difficult to detect. People do not suddenly drop dead or become ill after standing, sitting or sleeping on a particular spot. The effect is gradual, involving a slow deterioration in health in those susceptible to such stresses. As a result, they often find it difficult to feel happy, energetic, emotionally stable and physically well. A strange reaction to certain buildings could be our bodies' attempt to tell us that something is wrong in terms of the earth's energy, and that it would be harmful for us to live in that place or spend a lot of time there. But often we ignore this warning, or have lost our ability to sense the signals at all.

Where Can It Occur?

Houses

People who live in houses above areas of geopathic stress often have disturbed sleep patterns: they may not be able to get to sleep or they wake frequently or suffer from strange dreams and wake up feeling tired and irritable. This can lead to ill health, a lack of tolerance for others and general feelings of depression. In this situation arguments with loved ones ensue and life becomes more and more difficult. Babies and children in such houses do not sleep well and this causes problems for both themselves and their parents. People in such houses often become ill, sometimes with very serious complaints. This is particularly true if the negative energy is focused around the bed, where we spend about a third of our time. Affected houses do not sell because prospective buyers feel 'there is something they don't like about the house, even though they can't put their finger on it'. In consequence the house stays empty and often deteriorates and becomes even harder to sell.

Several years after buying such a house the owners may well say, 'I have never felt well since I lived in this house,' or 'Things have not gone right for me since we moved here.' Perhaps they talk about their own ill health or inability to sleep since they moved, or about problems for other family members. In desperation they may decide to move again. The house may see a constant turnover of owners because people cannot settle there or they decide to move in order to feel well, although their neighbours either side may stay for a long time. In such houses there is sometimes a history of cancer or other serious illnesses.

Some roads continually have houses for sale. In this case a whole area seems to be affected by something. People who live in these houses may become ill; babies could be born with birth defects; and people are perhaps more prone to being irritable, leading to quarrels, marital breakdowns and unhappiness. These streets or houses sometimes get the reputation for being unlucky places to live, but nobody knows why. Certain houses may become difficult to sell because of their reputation, and sometimes there will be a whole series of estate agents' signs in a particular road.

Geopathic stress can affect the fabric of a building. Pavements and walls can crack, plaster become damp and light bulbs blow for no apparent reason. The exasperated home owner may spend time and money repairing the damp, take the advice of experts, but still see the problem return for no obvious reason. The electric wiring can be checked and re-checked but the light bulbs may continue to blow with frequent and monotonous regularity. Attempts to decorate some rooms seem doomed to failure: they always seem gloomy and 'not quite right' no matter what is done. In spite of a new coat of paint and cheerful decorations no one wants to spend long in the room – and they cannot explain why.

Shops

Shops do not prosper if built on geopathically stressed ground because prospective customers will not want to stay on the premises; instead of browsing they will quickly leave if they do not see what they want. Indeed customers will often leave without really looking at anything. In some shops geopathic problems are more localized and only one particular area is affected, which is often 'dead' from a sales point of view.

Some shops will continually change hands even though the owner has worked hard and the business is in the right place. Often, similar businesses, a short distance away, may well succeed and flourish. If the owner becomes ill, this is usually put down to the stress of starting a new and struggling business. It remains a mystery why no one can make a success of this particular shop. People may decide that it is 'jinxed' in some way as prospective buyers become less and less willing to take it on – but perhaps there is another explanation.

Offices

Some offices are known as being difficult places to work in, although no one is quite sure why. These places probably have a high turnover of staff, and many of those who do stay are frequently ill, so that absentee and sickness rates are high. If a firm has several branches, the problems of this particular office will be contrasted with the success of those in other locations. Firms can spend vast sums of money on trying to find out what is wrong. They may change branch managers, bring in mechanical engineers to look at the air conditioning and heating, employ experts to examine the possibility of sick building syndrome, try different ways of organizing the work load, and ask consultants to interview the staff – but nothing works. In the end, head office may either decide that the people in this particular location are 'difficult' and do not want to work, or continue to be puzzled and feel the problems are intractable.

Geopathic stress can be seen as one aspect of sick building syndrome – or building-related illness as some people prefer to call it – which occurs when people become ill because of the building they work or live in. However, most people working in this field do not recognize geopathic stress as a contributing factor. In fact, in 1993, when I spoke at an engineering conference on indoor air pollution, of the 60 or so engineers present only one had heard of geopathic stress. (See Appendix for a fuller discussion of sick building syndrome.)

In late 1991 I was invited to visit an office block in the City of London by a mechanical engineer. I had previously talked to him about my work and he was interested to see what, if anything, I would deduce from examining this particular situation. Sick building syndrome had been mooted as the problem, but no conclusive evidence could be found. There was a high incidence of sickness throughout the building, and a rather mysterious build up of dust on computer screens. The air conditioning had been overhauled to no avail. The equipment and personnel of the cleaning contractors had been examined, and proved adequate for the job. When I checked the building I found a large Z of negative energy running through it, which I plotted on a floor plan of the building. (See *figure 1*, which is reproduced by permission of the *Journal of Alternative and Complementary Medicine*.) One of the angles of the Z contained particularly turbulent detrimental energy, located within one of the City's deal-

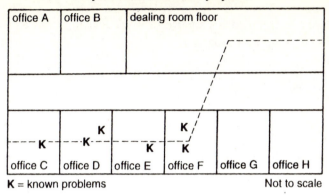

Figure 1 Central London dealing room floor: negative energy path

ing room floors. Although the floor was crowded with dealers on the morning of my visit, neither the mechanical engineer nor myself saw a single dealer standing in this area. Other parts of the Z went through offices, and the personnel officer confirmed that nearly all the sick people were located directly on this line. The other angle of the Z occurred in an office which was particularly known for its high sickness rate. It soon became clear that there was a similar problem on the floor above. Also, although many women were employed in these offices, the incidence of pregnancy appeared to be very low. Later I learnt that a firm on one of the higher floors also had lots of problems with staff sickness. But in view of my understanding that geopathic energies emanate from the earth and can travel upwards through concrete and other solid materials, I was not surprised. One other thing I noticed was that a colony of feral cats (animals which respond positively to geopathic stress) was occupying an area just outside the building, but still directly along the line of the Z.

Hospitals

Patients in hospital beds where geopathic stress is a problem are likely to suffer more post-operative complications and take longer to get well. In these circumstances, the environment needs to be as ideal as possible, but geopathic stress can undermine patients' energy and sleep patterns, thus delaying their recovery and hindering their progress.

Classrooms

Children whose desks happen to be placed over negative energy spots will find it difficult to concentrate in school; they are likely to become distracted and either over-active or lethargic, resulting in poor marks, disruption for other pupils and stress and frustration for the teacher. If a large area of the classroom is affected, many of the children may find it difficult to learn and some are likely to be frequently absent from school with various health problems. This type of situation may be blamed on the teacher, with adverse comments being made about the discipline and achievements of the children. Because the teacher would also be subject to the effects of these negative energy forces, he or she would not be in the best position to cope with the class.

Roads

It is well known that some roads have accident black spots. Sometimes there is an obvious explanation, such as poor visibility at a crossroad, but sometimes there is no apparent reason. Cars may have accidents there without any other vehicle being involved. Often the driver cannot explain why the accident occurred. 'Something just happened,' will be their puzzled answer. Undoubtedly, some of these will be freak accidents, but it is possible that in some cases geopathic energies temporarily interfere with the driver's concentration or vision with disastrous results.

Can Other Life Forms Be Affected?

Animals

Not all life responds to geopathic stress in the same way. While most humans are adversely affected by it, and some animals (such as dogs and horses) tend not to thrive if they live in a stressed area, other animals (such as cats, ants, wasps and beetles) respond in a different manner. For them it is a positive rather than a negative and detrimental force.

A client once consulted me about various health problems and I found that geopathic stress was part of the trouble. I asked her if she had a cat, but was told that she did not. However, she then added that all the local cats spent a lot of time in her garden. I gave her detailed instructions as to what she needed to do to her house to overcome the GS problems. When I saw her the next time, she remarked that not only was she feeling better, but also that the cats had stopped frequenting her garden. Presumably, once the negative energies had been corrected, the cats were no longer attracted to the area.

Dogs seem to thrive in the presence of the same type of energies as humans, so if you have a dog it would be a good idea to place your bed in a room directly over where the dog prefers to sleep. Other animals, such as pigs, cattle and horses, also respond to geopathic energies in the same way as human beings.

While I was treating a client for her health problems she told me about a problem she was having with one of her horses, which kept re-absorbing its foetus. This was both distressing and expensive in stud fees. A check of the stable showed that there was high geopathic energy within it, but that some nearby stalls were fine. The horse was moved to one of these stalls and given some minerals as a supplement. Next time the mare gave birth to a healthy foal.

Dr Joseph Kopp of Switzerland has spent some time looking at how animals are affected by geopathic stress. His initial work was with cows, and he looked at the earth energies of 130 barns which had housed sickly animals. In all cases he found that negative energy lines ran beneath the barns, often crossing the exact spot where the cows were tethered.[5]

Plants

Plants, like animals, respond to GS in different ways: some thrive in its presence, while others struggle to live and grow. Plants such as roses, azaleas, privet and celery tend not to do well in areas of geopathic stress, but asparagus, mushrooms, oak trees and elderberry will usually respond with increased growth and vigour. Taking into account what should grow well in a particular area, a look at which plants and trees are thriving in a garden may well give some clue as to whether or not there is a problem with geopathic stress in the house.

A plant may not thrive even though all the growing conditions are right, but on being moved to a different spot, even though all the conditions appear to remain the same, it suddenly starts to grow and blossom. Sometimes trees grow with gnarled and twisted trunks, or lean in a particular direction, even though this is not necessarily the direction of the light or wind. On occasions they may refuse to grow at all and wither and die, even though trees near them are doing well. Fruit trees may blossom but not set fruit, and the conscientious gardener will be at a loss to explain what has happened. Certain plants may not grow at all well in a particular spot in spite of what appear to be textbook conditions, while other plants which are known to be difficult to grow in those conditions may thrive beyond all expectation.

Moulds

Kopp also did work with foodstuffs and showed that jam became mouldy faster and wine soured more quickly when kept above an area of geopathic stress. This research suggests that the microbes which spoil food proliferate in the presence of detrimental earth energies.[6] Incidentally, it has been suggested that a compost heap *should* be located over a geopathic zone because then the vegetation will rot down more quickly.

It can be seen that geopathic stress affects all aspects of our lives, and also that of many animals and plants. Almost any illness can have a geopathic component, depending on the interrelation of the different ways in which geopathic stress can affect individuals. However, geopathic stress has been particularly implicated in cases of ME (post-viral syndrome), sleep problems, headaches, hyperactivity, allergies and some cancers. Infertility, birth defects and repeated miscarriages may also have a geopathic component, with the baby being affected either in the womb or because of malformation of the sperm or egg.

Often, living or working over a geopathically stressed zone would appear to hasten the onset of a chronic illness. In other words, although the symptoms of the disease will eventually develop anyway, ongoing exposure to geopathic stress may escalate the problem. Sometimes in this situation, people gradually become weaker in many different ways, exhibiting a whole host of symptoms and complaints. Sadly, these people are often regarded as neurotics or hypochondriacs by the medical profession and their family and friends. This adds to their overall stress levels as they feel that no one really understands, and their symptoms may well increase and their health become more and more compromised.

2

Geopathic Stress and Electromagnetism

Geopathic energies have probably always been there, but a central theme of this book is that we are becoming more susceptible to them, principally because of some of the technological changes now taking place. But unfortunately the ethos behind much modern technology means that many people are unwilling to consider the possibility of harm from sources which cannot as yet be measured accurately. In order to understand how these man-made changes could be disturbing the earth's natural energies, it is necessary to have some knowledge of electricity and magnetism.

THE ELECTROMAGNETIC SPECTRUM

Electromagnetic radiation has always been part of man's environment: sunlight and the earth's natural magnetic field existed long before man. The human species has evolved and developed in harmony with this background energy; in fact, it is essential for good health. For example, many medical studies have shown that without adequate sunlight people can suffer from rickets as a result of vitamin D deficiency. And during the winter months some people suffer from depression and lack of energy, which has now become known as Seasonal Affective Disorder (SAD). Treatment with full spectrum light has been shown to be beneficial. Ultraviolet light can also be used in a positive way to kill bacteria and has been found useful in the treatment of some cases of psoriasis, a painful and distressing skin disease. However, with the increasing concern about skin cancer, sunlight with its ultraviolet component is now being seen as a problem. With the destruction of the ozone layer, which may be because of some of the chemicals we use, more ultraviolet is reaching the earth and it is this that is leading to an increase in skin cancer. So we cannot live without sunlight, but because of modern technological developments it is beginning to have a negative impact on our lives. The same may well be true of energies other than light. They too may have harmful effects which are only now slowly beginning to be understood and, as with the problem of sunlight, this concern has partly come about as a result of modern technology.

Sunlight is only a part of the electromagnetic spectrum, as are radio waves and microwaves, but what are these waves? They are a combination of travelling electric and magnetic fields, carrying energy from one place to another, from the source to a receptor. Waves can be seen as travelling packets of energy. Electromagnetic energy is a combination of electrical and magnetic energy. Electromagnetic waves consist of perpendicular coupled electric and magnetic fields that travel through space at the speed of light. These differ from mechanical waves (such as sound, water, springs) which are caused by disturbance in a physical medium (for example, water, the string of a musical instrument). Light itself is an electromagnetic radiation, part of the electromagnetic spectrum.

The different waves have different wavelengths; waves with a shorter wavelength have a higher frequency. (See *figure 2*.) The whole range of frequencies forms the electromagnetic spectrum. Different waves also have different characteristics. For example, some parts of the spectrum can be seen – the visible light spectrum with which we are all familiar – whereas others cannot. We are also aware of the infra-red energy from a fire or an oven

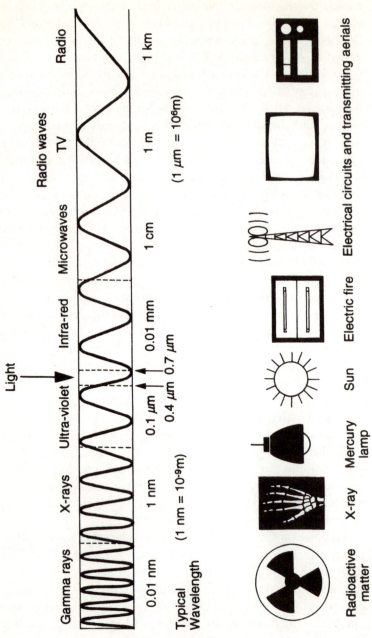

Figure 2 The electromagnetic system

because of the heat that is given out. Modern technology can display waves on a monitor such as an oscilloscope, giving a pictorial representation of their shape. Radio waves can cook for us (microwaves) and be encoded to transmit sound and pictures. Each energy type affects people in different ways. For example, gamma rays, which are of very high frequency, are given out by substances such as uranium. These rays are very dangerous to human beings because they can damage cells, causing chemical changes leading to severe illness and even death. However, x-rays, which are somewhat longer and of lower frequency, while also potentially damaging, can help save lives when used in the right way.

Electrical and magnetic fields

Electrical and magnetic fields surround us, acting in an unseen way. Various types of electromagnetic waves permeate the atmosphere. For instance, microwaves are used for satellite communication, radar detection devices and telemetry (remote switching of water pumps, machinery, sewage works, electricity substations and so on) as well as in microwave cookers. Television waves use separate frequencies for transmitting pictures, sound and teletext. Radio waves, television waves and microwaves travel through space and through our body tissues. This applies whether or not an individual is close to these appliances. However, if you are close to an electricity substation or a television, the effect is greater. Many people seem to think that if they do not have televisions or computers they are avoiding electromagnetic pollution from these sources. This is not true as the transmissions are happening all the time, even without an appliance to turn these electromagnetic waves into sound and pictures. In considering the machines in our homes we need to understand that the electrical field is there even when they are not being used. The current travelling along the electrical wires produces an electrical field and a magnetic field is produced at right angles to the wire. The magnetic field is only there when the appliance is switched on and electricity is running through the connecting wires. In other words, when you are using an appliance there is both an electrical and a magnetic field.

ELECTROMAGNETIC POLLUTION

Undoubtedly, in some areas our health has improved dramatically. Because of improved heating, sewage disposal and hygiene, we now live longer, and some diseases, such as tuberculosis, are becoming rare. Many of these improvements have come about partly as a result of the development of electricity. Yet the possible negative effects of this dependence on electricity are only just beginning to show. It is hard for many people to grasp that things which we cannot see, and about which our knowledge is so limited, can have a detrimental effect on our health. The negative effects of electricity are usually referred to as electromagnetic pollution, or electromagnetic smog. Under the combined onslaught of electromagnetic pollution and geopathic stress, human bodies show their frailty and start to lose their own electromagnetic integrity. Some people could probably cope with one of these phenomena without producing symptoms, but the two together submit the body to a negative energy overload that is hard to resist. In such circumstances it becomes increasingly difficult to stay well.

Without electricity and magnetism we would not have television, hi-fi systems, radios, computers, telephones, electric lights and many other modern-day conveniences. A power cut reminds us all very quickly of how dependent our lives have become on electricity. Also, in our homes there are many magnets, although we are largely unaware of their existence: there is usually one in fridge doors to create a firm closure; hi-fi speakers and telephone earpieces are dependent on them for their proper functioning; and many burglar alarms incorporate them as part of their warning system. The brown strip on the back of credit cards is magnetic, allowing information to be encoded on it and read by machines designed for that purpose. Computer disks, videotapes and audiotapes also contain tiny magnets. When the computer information, television programme or music is placed

Geopathic Stress and Electromagnetism 19

in these magnets, they are re-aligned into a pattern which is then fixed into the tape and can be read by the same or another machine. For this reason, credit cards and computer disks must be kept away from magnets, as they could inadvertently re-align the small magnets in the tape and destroy the information.

Electricity, produced by power stations, is distributed via the national grid to homes, factories and offices throughout the country. In the UK, power stations produce electricity at a voltage of 25,000 V (25 kV). This voltage is increased further by step-up transformers to 400 kV. Electricity at this voltage is carried by enormous pylons with very good insulation, because it is potentially lethal. These high voltages are used because they allow electricity to be carried in the most efficient way, minimizing heat and, therefore, energy loss. As the power nears towns, step-down transformer stations reduce the voltage to 132 kV. At this point the electricity can be carried by smaller pylons or, where appropriate, underground cables. At substations the voltage is reduced even further: to 230 V for lines to residential houses (110 V in the USA). The value of 230 V is considered to be a compromise between safety levels and the efficient transportation of electricity within the home (it is possible to survive an electric shock from 230 volts, but not from anything higher). Once in homes the electricity travels via the ring main to the various sockets. This electricity can then be used to run the many systems and appliances that are dependent on it. Even the car is an electrically-operated machine, with many of its functions relying on electricity, including a high voltage current to provide the spark to fire the engine. Also, whenever an electric current flows, a magnetic field is produced at right angles to the wire. It seems likely that it is this magnetic field, rather than the electrical field, that has the most negative effect. In fact, anything that plugs into an electrical supply and most things that contain a battery generate an electromagnetic field (EMF). The use of electricity and magnetism has brought us many benefits, but it may be that only now are we becoming aware of the price we have to pay for them.

As we have already seen, many of our body processes have an electrical or magnetic component. So we have to consider if it is possible for these processes to be influenced by external sources. We know that electromagnetic waves do not stop at the skin but penetrate the body. In fact the human body acts like a receiver. This can be shown very simply using a television set. If the normal aerial is removed, the picture deteriorates. However, if you put a finger over the aerial socket, the picture immediately improves. Reception is not as good as with the aerial, but this demonstration does show that the television waves in the air can be conducted through the physical body into the television set. Even without being connected to the television, these waves are present in our bodies.

During the Cold War the USSR actively transmitted an electromagnetic signal, aimed at US embassies throughout the world. It was known as the Woodpecker because of the woodpecker-like noise or interference it caused on radio receivers. This had a detrimental effect on many embassy staff, leading to anxiety attacks, irritability and nausea. The Woodpecker has even been implicated in some cases of leukaemia.

With the increasing use of electricity in our lives, the possibility of damage from these sources increases. So while we already know that x-rays can be dangerous and have set in place adequate precautions to protect both the people who administer them and the recipients, the effects of emissions from power lines, radio waves and other sources are largely ignored.

Electromagnetic radiation can be either ionizing or non-ionizing. Ionizing radiation, such as x-rays and that emitted by radioactive uranium, is known to be harmful to human beings because the high energy can break open molecules, tearing off electrons and forming ions. Microwaves, for example can vibrate molecules and cause heat, so are potentially dangerous through direct exposure. Microwaves pass through many things, including our bodies. The mechanisms by which these energies harm the human body are readily understood by scientists, and the possible dangers acknowledged. Extremely low frequency waves (ELFs), such as those emitted from power lines and electrical circuits, do not tear molecules apart or vibrate them. As current scientific knowledge does not provide us with any understanding of how these ELFs could damage living organisms, many scientists are unwilling to accept the possibility that this could happen. Yet it would be wrong to say that, because we have no understanding of the way in which a thing could happen, it cannot happen. We do not have enough evidence to be certain one way or the other.

The safety of electromagnetic fields

When we hear that the levels of the electromagnetic fields to which we are exposed are safe, it is wise to remember that this was said of x-rays in the early days of their use. The economic repercussions of accepting that EMFs are harmful would be immense. Many authorities are likely only reluctantly to accept that there is a link. We do not yet have absolute or even substantial proof of the role of EMFs in illness, but the evidence is mounting and the wise response surely is to err on the side of caution.

In 1992 the National Radiological Protection Board reviewed the evidence on electromagnetic fields and the risk of cancer. Although the report argued that many of the studies supporting such a link were flawed in some way, the Board urged that many more rigorous studies were necessary, and went on to say:

> It cannot be concluded either that electromagnetic fields have no effect on the physiology of cells, even if the fields are weak, or that they produce effects that would, in other circumstances, be regarded as suggestive of potential carcinogenicity.[7]

Science, however, still has only limited understanding of the phenomena of electricity and magnetism. In earlier centuries both magnetism and electricity were thought to be caused by fluids. This view is now clearly recognized as incorrect, but this does not mean that the modern scientific understanding of electricity and magnetism is totally correct. Scientific theory is constantly changing in the light of new evidence and new thinking. Although modern science on the whole does not accept that electromagnetic fields can cause harm, this is largely because such a notion does not fit in with currently accepted models. But it may be that it is these models that are flawed, rather than the claim that electromagnetic fields are damaging to human health.

Whenever you use electricity a magnetic field is generated. Although electrical fields can be shielded by barriers such as walls, magnetic fields can travel through walls, and only substances like lead will stop them. Thermal damage from electricity is readily acknowledged: faulty microwave ovens can cook people as well as food, and people regularly die from electric shocks from wrongly wired appliances. It is the non-thermal effects from properly functioning equipment that are much more in dispute, particularly the level at which the effects become harmful. Exposure to these waves over a long period of time may in fact prove to be harmful in a serious but less dramatic way than exposure to ionizing radiation and the higher non-ionizing frequencies.

Power lines

It is possible to measure the density of magnetic fields scientifically, in nanoteslas (nTs). One nT is equivalent to one thousandth of a millionth of a Tesla. The average household level is 70 nT. Tests have shown that the level below power lines can be as high as 1,000 nT. This is rather startling when it is recognized that even the 'normal' household level is an abnormal load on us. The first study showing a link between childhood cancer and power lines was published in 1979,[8] and there have been numerous studies since, not all of them confirming the link. In the USA some states have now set limits for the nanotesla measure in houses near power lines, and in Sweden the National Industrial and Technical Board (NUTEK) has advocated restrictions on building power lines close to houses until the dangers have been assessed more fully. There have also been claims that living close to power lines either exacerbates or causes headaches, depression, allergies, insomnia and irritability.

Computers and visual display units

There is now a growing sense of unease about the effects of computer visual display units (VDUs). These have been linked to eye strain, migraine and, more seriously, to miscarriages and birth defects. VDUs give out low levels of radiation across a wide range of frequencies. In a booklet produced by the London Hazards Centre the authors write:

> Electromagnetic radiation at either ionising or non-ionising frequencies is virtually impossible to measure accurately in the office and at the low levels concerned. Different frequencies need different methods of measurement, and at extremely low frequencies the instruments themselves can interfere with and distort the fields that they are measuring.

The same booklet says:

> . . . depending on the layout of the room, people who spend no time at all at a VDU may actually have higher exposure than those working on the screen: many VDUs emit more radiation from the side and back than from the front.[9]

In Simon Best's review of a whole range of studies on VDUs,[10] he showed that some emit higher levels of radiation than others. He too makes the point that radiation from the back of VDUs may be more serious than from the front of screens. Some of the studies which have not found a statistically significant link between working with VDUs and illness have ignored this fact and calculated exposure only from the front. Powerwatch UK, an information and campaigning organization on electromagnetic pollution, suggests that it is advisable to sit at least 4 feet away from the *back* of a computer monitor. They also advise that low radiation monitors meeting the Swedish legislation standards should be used. Simon Best also advised that light emitting diode (LED) screens should be used rather than the conventional cathode ray tube (CRT) screen. Anne Silk, an ophthalmologist, has reported that high oxygen-permeable lenses show distortions after their wearers have worked at VDUs for seven hours or more.[11]

There is obviously a real problem in trying to convince people of the harm that these emissions can do. One of the major problems is that the benefits of electricity are clearly evident in the form of our more comfortable and easier lives. The detrimental effects, if they exist, are much more difficult to see.

Steve Eabry, in an article in the September 1989 issue of the *International Journal of Alternative and Complementary Medicine*, states that 'a tremendous body of knowledge has been amassed' to demonstrate the dangers of man-made electric and magnetic fields, 'including increased tumour growth, many stresses and emotional problems, problems with foetal development, and it would seem, probably even cancer'. Roger Coghill, in another article in the same journal, describes various presentations at the 1989 American Bioelectromagnetic Society meeting in the USA. Coghill points out that much needed research is hampered by lack of funds. Even so, he found mounting scientific evidence for the danger of low frequency electromagnetic waves.

However, in a survey of the evidence in *Which? Way To Health* (December 1992), it is pointed out that the incidence of cancer has not risen as electricity consumption has increased. The article concludes: 'Until we have stronger grounds for concern, there is no reason to change our everyday use of electricity because of worries about EMR [electromagnetic radiation].'

Similar bland remarks were also made in the early days of investigation into the effects of nicotine consumption and the long-term use of the contraceptive pill. When we consider the vast amounts of money spent on finding cures for cancer, with only limited success, it is tempting to wonder if much of this research is misdirected. If even a small proportion of the money currently spent on looking for drugs to cure cancer was spent on research into electromagnetic fields, rapid progress could, perhaps, be made. Unfortunately most work in this area is privately funded: drug companies have no commercial interest in looking at EMFS and, unfortunately, most cancer charities seem very wedded to the medical and scientific establishment.

Sensitivity to electromagnetic phenomena

To complicate matters even further, it may well be that only certain people are susceptible to problems from EMFs. Even these people are not necessarily sensitive to all EMFs. In a study entitled *Electrical Sensitivities in Allergy Patients*, Dr V S Choy and his colleagues found that some of their allergy patients were sensitive to specific frequencies rather than to specific intensities. They found that the mechanism for *switching off* these sensitivities was the same as the one they would use for foods and chemicals. In my practice I have found that people who appear to be sensitive to many foods, chemicals, inhalants and contact substances are also very sensitive to geopathic and man-made electromagnetic phenomena. The apparent 'allergies' are in fact low tolerance levels for these substances. When patients' sensitivity to these negative energies is reduced, their tolerance for a wide range of substances frequently increases dramatically. This is particularly likely in people who are suffering from ME.

The attitude to the possibility of risk is slowly changing. At one time all scientific and medical authorities felt that EMFs presented no problem. However, in July 1994 it was accepted by an American court that an aluminium worker, James Brewer, had contracted cancer as a result of working in a foundry smelting aluminium from 1969 to 1986. This process uses high levels of electrical power. In his evidence Mr Brewer said that several other employees at the plant had developed lymphoma or leukaemia, with fatal results. His doctor said that it was 'more probable than not' that his cancer was caused by exposure to EMFs through his job.[12]

It is clearly unrealistic to try to go back to a time when mankind did not use electricity and magnetism, but it is important that this area of growing concern is fully investigated.

3

Types of Geopathic Energy

Having seen how electromagnetic pollution may be making us more susceptible to the effects of geopathic stress, we now need to look more closely at earth energies and how they manifest themselves.

There are many different types of negative earth energies, each having its own particular characteristics. It is important that all the different types are considered when checking an area. It has been found that when testing for geopathic energies it is insufficient to have only a general, vague concept of detrimental negative energy. The process seems to be akin to tuning a radio. It is not enough simply to tune the radio in some undefined way; you have to know the frequency of the station you are trying to find. Looking at it another way, there are many different energies within the universe and a skilled dowser or kinesiologist can undoubtedly find many of these. In order to find the geopathic ones it is necessary to have a clear definition and 'feel' for what is involved, otherwise there is a risk of being overwhelmed and distracted by all the other energies occupying the same space. The practitioner's understanding of these energies influences what is found: the clearer and more comprehensive the understanding, the more accurate the testing.

Many different aspects of energy can be described in scientific terms (frequency, coherence, amplitude, direction, spin, charge

Types of Geopathic Energy

and so on). Unfortunately it is as yet impossible to analyse geopathic energy in this way, so the differentiation of geopathic types remains an experiential one, based, that is, on the awareness and perceptions of the practised observer. It is impossible to convey a full understanding of the characteristics and feel of the different types of geopathic energies; it is necessary to develop an awareness of them under the guidance of an experienced and knowledgeable practitioner.

Water

Many people interested in geobiology concentrate entirely on detecting underground water. Water is an important phenomenon, but not the only one. In general, the faster water flows, and the greater the volume of water flowing, the greater the geopathic effect. Where water suddenly changes levels, as happens where there are changes in geological strata, geopathic problems are likely to be more intense, particularly at sites over a spot where two underground streams cross, even if there is a considerable depth variation between them. Where underground water causes geopathic problems it seems to give rise to negative energy. However, underground water does not always cause problems. Water that is negative in this way is often referred to as 'black water' or 'black streams'. Confusingly, some dowsers use these terms to refer to any geopathic energy, regardless of whether it originates with water. It is important, therefore, to check what definition any writer or speaker is using. Water above ground, for instance a river or a lake, does not usually cause problems.

Curry Lines

Curry lines are a global, grid network of electrically charged lines of natural origin. These lines, as *figure 3* shows, run diagonally to the poles (NE-SW and SE-NW), and were first discovered by Dr Manfred Curry and Dr Wittmann. There is some

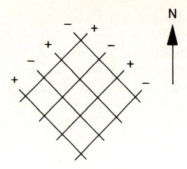

Figure 3 Curry grid

disagreement between authorities as to how wide apart these lines are, but the consensus seems to be approximately 3 metres; although most experts recognize that this can vary. The lines themselves are not seen as a problem, only the points where they cross, and obviously lines which run in this way will have numerous intersecting points. As the lines are electrically charged, the intersecting points are either double positives, double negatives or one of each. From his studies Dr Curry felt that the positively charged spots lead to a proliferation of cells, with the possibility of cancerous cell growth, whereas the negatively charged spots could lead to inflammation.

Hartmann Lines

The Hartmann net (*figure 4*) also consists of naturally occurring charged lines, running N-S and E-W. It is named after Dr Ernst Hartmann who first described it. Alternate lines are usually positively and negatively charged, so where the N-S and E-W lines cross it is possible to have double positive charges, double negative charges, or one positive and one negative charge. Once again it is the intersections that are seen as a source of potential problems.

It has been suggested that both the Curry and Hartmann lines are earthing grids for cosmic rays, and that they can be distorted

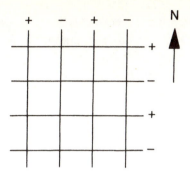

Figure 4 Hartmann net

by other things, such as geological fault lines and underground mining. It is also possible to have spots where the Curry and Hartmann lines cross, causing further potential problems. These spots are generally seen to be more detrimental than a single crossing within the Hartmann or Curry system.

Black Lines

Black lines seem to be naturally generated, although quite how is not known. They may be localized and do not form a network in the same way as Hartmann and Curry lines. Black lines can be straight or curved, at ground level or even higher up – they may be evident on the upper floors of buildings, but not on the lower floors. An unskilled person may miss these lines if only looking at the ground to find energy disturbances. There seem to be several different types of black lines. Someone who is able to 'see' these energies described one type as black and depressed, another as shiny, black, hard and sharp.

There is a tendency to think that geopathic energies are always in lines or streams. And, unfortunately many practitioners in this field are only able to conceptualize energy in this way. Consequently they miss many of the energies that can affect people adversely. In dowsing and kinesiology (see Chapter 6), concepts and assumptions are of vital importance. Important energies can unwittingly be excluded because the practitioner's definitions do not include the possibility of finding an energy with those characteristics.

Spots and Spirals

Some geopathic energies occur as spots or spirals. Spirals can have the energy flowing in towards the centre or out towards the periphery. They can be spiralling into the ground or out of it. In all cases, although the shape of the spiral is the same, the energy effects are different. Spots are usually randomly located on their own, whereas spirals usually occur in pairs. However, they are not necessarily together and only one of the spirals may be found when looking at a particular area because the other is a little way away and not within the perimeter of the site.

Energy Clouds or Fog

An energy cloud or fog seems only to occur inside buildings. It appears to be energy which is trapped within the structure in some way, although it can go through walls and ceilings. A cloud is usually about 10 feet wide. Perhaps it would be more accurate to describe it as a function of the building and the relationship between walls. In this sense the cloud does not emanate from the earth, but is caused inadvertently, usually by man-made structures that do not allow energy to flow adequately. Psychically an energy cloud has the qualities of an immature energy without clear boundaries, shape or form. People who can see these things say it 'looks' like smoke or fog, with a slightly fluttering quality to it. This does not seem to be a particularly detrimental form of energy, probably, at least partially, because it is often located in stairwells and similar places where people do not spend a lot of time. It has been suggested that people are more likely to trip and have an accident in a stairwell if an energy cloud is located there.

Schumann Waves

Schumann waves are naturally occurring, beneficial electromagnetic waves that oscillate between the earth and certain layers of the atmosphere. They were first identified in 1952 by Professor W O Schumann, a German scientist. He found that these waves have almost the same frequency as brain waves and follow a similar daily pattern. It has been suggested that these waves help regulate the body's internal clock, thus affecting sleep patterns, hormonal secretions, the menstrual cycle in women and so on. The American space agency NASA became interested in this phenomenon when the early astronauts returned to earth after only a short time in space feeling distressed and disorientated. Subsequently NASA installed equipment to generate Schumann waves artificially in their spacecraft.

Some modern buildings with reinforced concrete and metal roofs can inadvertently shield occupants from these beneficial waves. Part of the reason why people suffer from jet lag is that the Schumann waves are much weaker at normal aeroplane altitudes, and this effect is further weakened by the metal fuselage.

Energy Drains

About two years ago, through using kinesiology, I discovered a phenomenon which I have named 'energy drains'. At first I was slightly puzzled as to its exact nature; only subsequently did I begin to understand more about it. In the locations studied in England and Canada these drains have been found roughly half a mile apart in every direction. They are not necessarily at ground level. In fact the first one I ever found was in mid-air in a room two floors up. I spent some time testing this and other energies that had a similar feel, and eventually came to the conclusion that they are in fact part of the normal structure of things. They are indeed intended to be there and are part of the energy system of the planet. The problem arises when they become 'blocked' in some way so that energy cannot drain freely through them. Any corrective activity should not involve removing them, because it seems that they are essential to the proper dispersal of energy from the physical world into some other dimension in some way that we do not as yet understand.

Dr Jimmy Scott, the founder of Health Kinesiology, has suggested that these drains may well act as safety valves. through which a build-up of energy can be safely dispersed. It is possible that there are different types relating to different forms of energy. Obviously, if they are not functioning properly the drains need to be cleared so that too much energy 'pressure' does not build up. The concept of energy drains seems very different from many other geopathic phenomena, which we usually wish to neutralize or inactivate in some way. When we consider energy drains we want to restore them to a pristine condition, rather than remove them. It may well be that a system of these drains covers the entire planet, playing an essential part in the ebb and flow of energy throughout creation. It seems likely that there are other similar mechanisms, forming part of the anatomy of the universe's subtle energy system. If this is the case, these structures too may cause problems when they are not functioning properly. I suspect that this may be a very fruitful area for research in the future.

Ley Lines

Ley lines are generally recognized as man-made phenomena, occurring where sacred stones, which have been charged energetically in some way, are laid in a straight line. You may hear people referring to all geopathic energies as ley lines, and this use is particularly misleading. A ley line appears 'naturally' and spontaneously if at least five such stones are placed in a line, with the two furthest stones no more than 25 miles apart. Often the charged stones are in the form of ancient standing stones and are quite spectacular, such as those found at Stonehenge and throughout Cornwall. Even small stones can be energetically charged, either by heating them in a fire or throwing them with considerable force against another rock. The blow or the heat seems to fix into the stone the energetic charge of the person or people involved so that it does not decay and disappear in the normal way. In their books both Lethbridge and Havelock Fidler give intriguing accounts of charging stones. Ley lines themselves are invisible and can stretch over many miles. Although usually at ground level, sometimes they are totally above ground. It is generally felt that ley lines have been created deliberately.

It has also been suggested that these lines were used by ancient people as a method of communication. This may seem improbable, but so would the idea of the telephone or e-mail two centuries ago. Ley lines may also have been used for delineating pathways and boundaries or for enhancing crop and animal fertility. When I encounter ley lines I am very much aware of the feel and quality of the people who made them. Ley line energy has a distinctly human personality to it!

In *Needles of Stone Revisited,* Tom Graves suggests that ancient man was simply amplifying existing earth energies, and he likens standing stones to a form of acupuncture of the earth. Most other authorities do not go along with this, believing rather that the makers of the ley lines were creating new energy lines that had not been there before. Some ley lines appear to have a negative effect on the people exposed to them. Possibly these were set up in order to remove an inappropriate energy from an area, or perhaps their initial benign use has in some way been distorted by later unintentional intervention by man. As Havelock Fidler says in his book *Ley Lines* (page 109):

> It has been pointed out that the activities of modern 'civilized' man are fracturing many existing ley lines. One only has to think of the effect of cutting a wide band across country for a modern motorway to realize what damage to the ley system must be constantly taking place.

It may be tempting to try to set up ley lines yourself, but Fidler rightly goes on to caution against this (page 118):

> As yet we have very little knowledge of the potential power for good or evil of this energy, although there are indications that it can be great. Until such time as we have this knowledge, it is very undesirable to add to or alter the existing system.

Emotionally Charged Stones

The fact that stones can be energetically charged by hitting them has profound implications for houses built of stone. Does this mean that houses built of dressed stone contain 'something' of the energy of the builder? In one case I found that the stone in a client's house did indeed appear in some way to contain a negative emotional vibration. On questioning her about this, I learnt that the builder had gone bankrupt shortly after finishing her house and, of course, he was likely to have known of his financial problems during the course of its construction. Possibly, then, the vibrational quality of his distress was in some way held in the stone of the house and could be felt in some subtle way by the people living there. In order for this to happen the builder's emotion would need to be intense and experienced over a significant period. If this theory is indeed correct, it is important to make sure that people who build houses are as happy and stress free as possible or, alternatively, that any negative energy charge is removed from the building on completion.

The Paranormal

No discussion of geopathic energies would be complete without a consideration of the paranormal. Strictly speaking, paranormal energies are not geopathic, but their effect can be very similar. There is much debate as to what exactly paranormal phenomena are, and whether such things even exist outside the imaginings of some rather hysterical or susceptible people. If, as seems likely, strong thought forms can in some way become attached to buildings, this may be an explanation for ghosts and other apparitions. Traumatic events may generate such intense emotions in a person that the energy vibration of these thoughts and feelings becomes imprinted in some way on the building and remains long after his or her death. In certain circumstances these thought forms may become re-enacted so that 'ghosts' appear. Again this may seem a fanciful notion but, as with the ley lines and e-mail analogy, we have a modern-day equivalent in the form of video films. It has also been suggested that ghosts occur when a person has died suddenly and the etheric body has in some sense been 'left behind'. Because of the different forms that paranormal phenomena may take, it is likely that there is no one single explanation for the exact mechanism for their activity. Whatever the origins of paranormal happenings, it is clear that some people react to them in an adverse way. Various techniques have been used to clear these energies and it is interesting to note that most of them (such as exorcism) also involve thought forms. It may well be that a strongly positive thought form is imposed on the negative thought form, cancelling out the negative effect.

Although I have discussed the various types of geopathic energies separately, it is quite common to have several different types of detrimental energies in the same building, interacting and affecting each other and together making things worse than the sum of the individual energies. Unfortunately, geopathic energies do not in general cancel each other out, but instead tend to exacerbate one another. Where several energies overlap the situation can be quite complex and make an understanding of the problem more difficult. When correcting geopathic energies it is usually better to consider the whole picture rather than dealing with individual types of energies.

4

How Geopathic Stress Affects the Body

Many people believe that viruses, bacteria and other foreign agents are responsible for illnesses, and see drugs and surgical intervention as the cure. However, as we are all constantly exposed to a wide assortment of hostile organisms, why are we not ill all the time? If germs *caused* illness, then every time we were exposed to one we would become ill, and this is clearly not the case. The simple answer is that the body can resist most organisms unless and until it is in some way weakened by other factors, and one such factor is stress.

OVERALL STRESS

The idea of stress as a major factor in ill health is now becoming widely accepted. Stress can take many forms and will exacerbate any situation, making the individual more prone to illness. And where there are inherited problems – for instance, medical evidence clearly shows that both asthma and eczema run in families – many sufferers know that any form of stress makes their symptoms even worse.

The body has a general response to stress. Dr Hans Selye, one of the leading authorities on the subject, calls this the General Adaptation Syndrome (GAS). Under stress of any kind, the physical body shows a specific physical response, regardless of whether the stress is emotional (a fight with a loved one), financial (loss of a job) or physical (lack of sleep or working in an environment which is consistently too cold or too hot). The body's response is controlled by hormones and, when under stress, a wide-ranging set of changes occur (GAS). The hypothalamus monitors the physical body and, through its connection to the cerebral cortex, an individual's psychological state. It initiates the changes necessary to counteract stress by instructing the pituitary gland which in turn tells the adrenal glands which hormones to release.

There are two parts to the body's reaction to stress: the alarm reaction and the resistance reaction. The alarm reaction is commonly referred to as the fight-or-flight response, because it initiates the bodily changes necessary to help us successfully run away or fight. The brain becomes very alert, blood pressure increases, breathing quickens and digestion, temporarily unimportant, is slowed. The second part of the GAS is the resistance reaction, which is slower to start and has longer-lasting effects. If the stress continues for some time, however, the body remains in a state of apprehension and tension. With time it becomes exhausted, because of the demands placed on the organs by the continuing resistance reaction. Gradually the body becomes more and more debilitated by the on-going effect of the stress and less and less able to handle it constructively. The person becomes ill. Blood pressure may remain inappropriately raised; excess acid may be produced by the stomach, leading to stomach ulcers; decreased activity by white blood cells will lead to less effective resistance to viruses and bacteria; and the person may have difficulty sleeping as the body is on continuous alert. In this situation the body is prone to develop new and more serious problems, as overall health becomes undermined. Reduced resistance leads to more frequent colds and flu which further undermine the body and cause a downward spiral of further illness and debilitation.

GEOPATHIC STRESS

Although the effects of stress are becoming more familiar, what is not so well documented is the true range of causes. Geopathic stress, for example, is usually ignored because most people are totally unaware of its presence. This type of stress is usually chronic, with exposure occurring every day, often for long hours as a person sleeps in a bed or sits in a chair above negative earth energies. The body is constantly fighting to cope with this ongoing stress by producing large quantities of the stress hormones. This has a debilitating effect on the body, leaving it more susceptible to bacteria and viruses and less able to cope with other eventualities.

The effects of geopathic stress undermine and weaken a person's life force. This does not mean that GS *causes* illness; rather, by weakening the body it provides a fertile ground in which ill health can flourish. As the body's defences become more stressed, the person, plant or animal is less able to resist viruses, bacteria, mould spores, atmospheric pollution and so on. It is the interaction of the two – a body weakened by geopathic stress and a virus – which causes the problem.

Scientific acceptance of geopathic energies faces three problems: does geopathic stress really exist, how can it be measured, and what is its mechanism for doing harm? Unfortunately, the evidence for the existence of GS is mainly anecdotal and can only be detected and measured in ways not yet accepted by conventional physics. In saying that geopathic energies are stressful to the body it is not known exactly how this effect occurs. Our understanding of the mechanisms for damaging health are at the moment speculative. Several different theories have been proposed by people working in this field, but as yet there is no consensus. It is almost certain that there are several different mechanisms involved.

The Subtle Energy System

An important mechanism by which the body is affected by geopathic stress is through what is known as the subtle energy system. This is central to the health of the individual. Damage at the level of the subtle bodies, particularly the etheric body, the chakras and the meridians (we will return to all these concepts in detail) can eventually lead to damage to the physical body. Both the internal subtle energies and the external subtle energies (such as geopathic stress) share many of the same characteristics. *It is likely that as our understanding and ability to measure the energy of the subtle bodies increase, this will be shown to be the primary mechanism for the effect of geopathic energies.* Given its importance, the subtle energy system will be looked at in depth in the following chapter.

The Body's Electrical System

Another explanation for how GS affects the body is that the geopathic energies interfere with the body's own electrical activity. We usually see electromagnetic waves as being outside ourselves, but this is far from the truth. For example, our bodies have a small amount of natural radioactivity: we actually contain radioactive isotopes of potassium-40, which emits beta particles and gamma rays. Dr C W Smith has described how some allergically sensitive people emit an electromagnetic signal at a level that can cause interference with electrical and electronic equipment.[13] This signal can be demonstrated by getting such a person to hold a plastic-cased tape recorder, with the record button pressed, but without a microphone in use. A variety of different sounds have been recorded in this way, some of them akin to those elicited from the type of fish that emit electrical impulses.

Also, the body itself contains many processes that are electrical. The brain, governing so much within our body, is basically electrical. When our heart beats, it produces small electrical pulses. We are able to move our arms and legs because electrical messages are sent from the brain, via our nerves, to our muscles. Nerves and muscles are electrically excitable. Muscles work by responding to electrical impulses from the brain via the nerves. Even dreaming involves electrical activity within the brain. We are truly electrical creatures: our bodies are electromagnetic generators.

Also, our tissues are good conductors of electricity: they have to be in order to allow the nerve messages, which are small bursts of electrical activity, to flow freely from the brain. Our bodies are generally recognized to be between 70 and 90 per cent water, and water is known to be a very good conductor of electricity. All body fluids are excellent electrical conductors. It may well be that this internal electrical activity and the conductivity of tissues make us more susceptible to external electrical and magnetic forces.

External electromagnetic fields can cause interference with television and radio reception, and it may be possible that they can also affect the workings of the human brain in some way. Disturbances in the outer magnetic field by geopathic energies could disturb our own inner electrical and magnetic processes, leading to illness and unhappiness.

Brain Rhythms

Peter Rivett in a short article in the Wessex Cancer Help Centre newsletter (June 1994) offers this theory:

> The effect of geopathic stress shows up in the distortion of brain rhythms. The alpha brain rhythm increases to about 15 herg and the corresponding beta rhythm to about 30 herg – getting closer to the 50 hg magnetic field generated by our power supply system. Geopathic stress appears to affect the body's housekeeping in the production of new cells and the immune system is weakened. Many affected people complain of not getting a good night's rest and of not having much energy. Because their immune system is below par they are hostage to ill health.

Cellular Renewal

We tend to think that once our bodies are fully developed they remain static, except perhaps for the changes which take place with age. Yet the body is continually renewing itself and after a period of time (between three and ten years) the whole body is replaced. Certainly the physical body you have now does not contain any of the atoms or molecules that you had fifteen years ago. The molecules are replaced so slowly that we have the illusion that our eyes and hands and face and internal organs are the same ones we had all those years ago. Although some evidence for this process is visible – hair and nails grow, skin flakes and peels – cellular renewal goes on unseen throughout the whole body. As Deepak Chopra writes in *Quantum Healing* (page 48):

> All of us are much more like a river than anything frozen in time and space. If you could see your body as it really is, you would never see it the same twice. Ninety-eight per cent of the atoms in your body were not there a year ago.

Chopra goes on to give figures for the rate at which various parts of the body change: the skin is replaced within a month, the stomach lining every four days, the liver is completely renewed every six weeks. Conventional medicine has no adequate explanation for the mechanism by which this is achieved: how the body knows how to replicate itself exactly and repeatedly. Alternative therapies postulate that this is the role of the etheric body, which is said to contain the blueprint for the physical body. This constant renewal of the body gives rise to the possibility for profound healing, but also represents an opportunity for damage and harm. One possibility is that geopathic energies can in some way interrupt this continuous process of renovation and renewal.

Resonance

Geopathic energies may cause damage to specific parts of the body more directly because they resonate at the same frequency as that particular organ or body part. Even a cursory look at the subject of geopathic stress suggests that there are many different types of geopathic energy, each with its own frequency. All objects have a natural frequency, which can be set in motion or increased by something nearby that is vibrating at the same frequency or pitch. When this happens we say that the two things have the same resonance. The idea that an opera singer can break a glass is based on this idea. The glass is affected by the note, starts to vibrate at the same frequency and eventually shatters. In the 1940s the Tacoma bridge in America collapsed because a cross-wind set up resonant vibrations in the structure, causing it to swing so much that it broke up. Resonance is the frequency at which maximum energy transfer takes place and can be seen in less spectacular form in everyday life: parts of a car rattle when the engine reaches a particular speed, and parts of a house rattle when heavy lorries go past. The vibration of one causes a resonant vibration of the other.

Things which vibrate quickly have a higher pitch. Different geopathic energies appear to vibrate at different frequencies, giving them their own unique qualities and ability to affect human beings. As with the opera singer and the glass, if the GS energy resonates at the same frequency as a body organ it can damage that organ. Every organ of the body has its own resonant frequency. When a person or a part of the body is in resonance with an electromagnetic wave, energy from the wave will be absorbed into the body. It is, of course, feasible that this energy will have a beneficial effect, but it is the nature of geopathic energies that they cause harm to the organ or tissues through which they pass. The greatest damage occurs when the maximum resonance is experienced. This explains why not everyone living or working in the same environment will be affected by the geopathic problems of the site.

In investigating geopathic energies I have found that some energies only affect women. The reason for this seems to be that a particular type of energy resonates at the same frequency as the ovaries. Although men are not directly affected by this energy, it may well be that they are affected in the more general overload sense (see next section). Also, not all women seem equally susceptible, which may mean that there is a frequency range for the ovaries, and women whose ovaries happen to be at exactly the same frequency as the detrimental energy are most affected. John Davidson in his book *Radiation* likens this effect to that of a key in a lock. The key only works if it is exactly the right size and shape. If the key does not fit, producing a larger key will not open the door. Similarly, it is the frequency of the energy that is important, rather than the strength.

Much of the focus for criticism of the work on geopathic and electromagnetic disturbances has tended to make the assumption that stronger frequencies have more effect. This, as the key analogy illustrates, is not necessarily the case. Dr C W Smith puts this clearly:

> Much of the present effort in looking for electric and magnetic field effects in biological systems involves the assumption that if the experiment is done, at, say ten thousand gauss [a measure of the strength of a magnetic field], one should obtain ten thousand times the effect [obtained] at one gauss. If nothing is found of the higher field, it is argued that there should be less than nothing at the lower field.[14]

Overload on Particular Body Parts

In addition to sympathetic resonance people can be affected in a particular part of their body because a negative energy line crosses that point while they sleep. When energy lines are plotted through a house it is interesting to see how often the negative line is located across the bed. Occasionally all of the bed is affected, but sometimes the line is more localized and the occupant will be exposed to negative forces in only a limited part of his or her body. And frequently this is where any affected organs or tissues will be located. Kathe Bachler's book *Earth Radiation* documents clearly many examples of this phenomenon. Christopher Bird in *The Divining Hand* (page 268) quotes the words of Herbert Douglas, an American dowser:

> I thought that the underground veins could be best illustrated if I laid out a series of wooden laths on the bed to show the direction of their flow. When I did this, I asked the person who slept in the bed to lie down in the position they normally assume when falling asleep. Repeatedly, the crossing of the laths indicates precisely where the person is afflicted.

The geopathic stress can produce illness by affecting a person's weakest point. If your throat is the weak link, you may well suffer from throat problems, whereas if your stomach is your weakest organ, digestive problems may appear. The effect of the stress will bring out any underlying weakness in the body.

The Body's Use of Magnets

Research has found that magnetite is present in a range of organisms, including humans. Magnetite is an iron ore and is naturally magnetic. It is also called lodestone and was used by sailors to help them navigate: a piece of magnetite was floated on wood in water and, as one end always pointed north, the ship's course could be charted from this. Magnetite has been found in both the adrenal glands and the brains of human beings. It has not as yet been established what role, if any, this serves in the organism. However, if, as is suspected, the magnetite is part of the message system of the body, this would begin to suggest yet another mechanism by which human health could be affected. Steve Eabry, in his review of the above research, writes:

> It must be recognised that here we have a system continually tuned into very low level magnetic fields, a sensitive receiver looking for information to pass on and utilise throughout the organism. Many, many tiny magnets throughout our brain, ethmoid bone and adrenals, looking for a DC (steady) signal, but instead being twitched by a 60 Hz (60 times a second) signal. It seems obvious that such interference from low strength, man-made fields (that is, at or less than the geomagnetic field or biologically generated field strengths) would be received by this system and would confuse it such that detrimental biological effects would be expected.[15]

Although Eabry is talking about man-made electromagnetic fields, this would also apply to geopathic stress, if this is, indeed, largely electromagnetic in origin. Further, William Philpott explains how 'there is clinical evidence justifying the conclusion that a negative magnetic field keeps the pH buffer system intact'.[16] This suggests that possibly an internal magnetic mechanism allows our bodies to maintain the correct acid-alkaline balance that is so important to our well-being. If this is so then it is possible that this delicate mechanism could be upset by external electromagnetic influences, including geopathic energies. Philpott also describes some interesting case studies using magnets to heal, particularly in diabetes. This shows how magnetic forces can be used to effect changes within the body. In this case the changes are, of course, beneficial.

Body Polarity

The unusual ideas of René Naccachian, a French engineer, are explained in an article by Ronnie Turner.

> He said the body worked like a battery. Every cell had to be connected to the negative-pole energy of the earth, coming upwards, and the positive-pole energy of the cosmos, coming downwards. Many people were 'disconnected' by geopathic stress. Energy then did not reach all cells and the weakest areas would deteriorate. Toxins and dead cells would not be eliminated.[17]

Blood Polarity

Richard Gerber in *Vibrational Medicine* recounts tests using a Vega machine and a Rotation Tester, which showed changes in the blood of those exposed to geopathic stress. It had been found that these individuals had a counterclockwise rotational polarity in their blood. On moving away from the detrimental energies, the blood eventually resumed its normal clockwise polarity. While their blood exhibited the abnormal polarity, these people also seemed resistant to treatment for any illness they were suffering from. Gerber goes on to say that it has been shown that many cancer sufferers exhibit this counterclockwise polarity when tested using a Vega machine.

Magnetic Sensitivity

Paul Devereux in *Places of Power* (pages 202–3) writes:

> It is now known, after a long period of scientific disbelief, that a whole variety of living systems can be sensitive to low levels of magnetism . . . Researchers have found that bacteria can respond to the North Pole or to a magnet moved around them . . . Other creatures scientifically tested and found to possess magnetic sensitivity include algae, crabs, salmon, honey bees, salamanders, robins, mice . . . The list of lifeforms sensitive to subtle levels of magnetism is now very long . . . If other organisms can detect magnetism, what about human beings?

Those who accept the power of homoeopathy will find nothing strange in the idea that very low level electromagnetic changes can cause health problems. Homoeopathy uses doses of substances that are too diluted to be assayed by normal means. Conventional scientists argue that homoeopathic medicines are diluted to the point where it would be impossible to have some of the original substance in each tablet without splitting atoms. Yet homoeopathy is gaining wider acceptance, as people see its efficacy not only for adults but also for small babies and animals. Many scientists would say there is no material dose of anything in the tablet, but the homoeopath would respond that the tablet contains the energetic pattern of the original substance and this works at levels other than that of the physical body.

Sensitivity to Geopathic Energies

Undoubtedly some people are more sensitive to geopathic stress in general. Also, because there are many different types of geopathic energies, each with their own characteristics, it is possible to be more sensitive to some of these energies than others. Therefore, when assessing the geopathic stress problems of a site, it is important to take into account people's *overall* sensitivity to negative earth energies as well as their sensitivity to the *particular* range of energies present.

We have seen that there are many possible mechanisms by which geopathic stress can affect our health. I am convinced that the major mechanism is that of a direct effect on the integrity of the subtle energy system in general, and the etheric body and the chakras in particular. The whole of the following chapter is devoted to a discussion of this complex and important subject.

Any sensitivity to negative earth energies is further increased if the person is exposed to other forms of stress. The evidence for humans being sensitive to electromagnetic pollution is mounting. With the increasing use of electricity in the form of computers, power lines, televisions and so on, the total electromagnetic load on people has increased, and many individuals now seem susceptible to much lower levels of geopathic stress. These people will exhibit symptoms sooner from a given level of exposure to geopathic energies if they have also been exposed to electromagnetic pollution. The frequencies we are considering with geopathic stress are likely to be much higher than those of the known electromagnetic spectrum, and here the problem of proof is much more difficult. Some scientists will now concede that power lines can have a detrimental effect on some people, but low level emissions from the earth, even if it is accepted that they exist, are often viewed as harmless.

Recognizing that the phenomenon of geopathic stress can profoundly affect a person's health and sense of well-being is not on its own sufficient. There are many causes of ill health, and geopathic stress may be a contributory factor in many cases. With the best care, either orthodox or alternative, susceptible individuals are unlikely to get well and stay well unless the geopathic stress energies are detected and corrected.

5

The Subtle Energy System

SUBTLE ENERGY

There appear to be energies beyond the 'ends' of the electromagnetic spectrum, and it is in this area beyond normal scientific understanding that some geopathic energies exist and have their effect.

Science, at the moment, does not have the means to detect these energies, but this does not mean that they do not exist. They are usually referred to as subtle energies. *The Concise Oxford Dictionary* defines subtle as 'tenuous or rarefied . . . evasive, mysterious, hard to grasp or trace . . . making fine distinctions'. Subtle energy is a loose term used to describe any energy which is not specifically recognized and categorized by conventional scientific knowledge. Some of these energies are seen as being part of man. Others are seen as being outside of the individual person and generated by completely separate sources. Geopathic energy is one of these.

The basic premise underlying this book is that a person's own energy system is undermined by detrimental energy coming from the earth. Geopathic energies are seen to directly affect some of the subtle energies that are part of an individual. Physical damage occurs as a result of damage to the more subtle energies of the body.

The Subtle Energy System

The subtle energy system has been extensively documented by photographing it with special apparatus. Kirlian photography, also known as electrography, was developed in Russia by Semyon Kirlian. Photographs are taken in the presence of a high frequency, high voltage, low amperage electrical field. This produces a halo around the object, said to represent its energy field. Kirlian photography shows that different halos are generated by organic and non-organic vegetables, and by sick and healthy people. It also claims to be able to provide information about a person's physical and emotional health based on photographs of the hands.

We tend to see the physical world as being made up of solid objects, but in reality even solid objects have spaces within them. There are gaps within and between the molecules that make up physical shapes. Atoms themselves are made up of apparently empty space. The reason we can see physical objects is because their vibrational rate is so slow that it gives the appearance of solidity. We cannot see microwaves, because the vibrational level is so high. So some people's insistence that they will only accept what they can see seems very limited and illogical. They cannot see sound, but they accept it because they use other receptors (ears) to establish its presence. Some of the things in this book cannot be understood through the normal way we process information, but this does not mean these things do not exist. Because someone is blind the physical world does not cease to exist. It is through the work of clairvoyants and others working in the area of subtle energy that these forces and phenomena are beginning to be described.

The concept of molecules and atoms paints a very different picture of the universe from the one we see in our everyday world. Molecules and atoms move in ways which we cannot observe with our eyes, but, none the less, this movement is real. Subtle energy is seen as existing within and beyond normal matter, forming a blueprint for physical reality. This subtle energy blueprint could well be the mechanism through which the body knows exactly how to grow, so that arms end up the same length and the body repairs itself when injured. John Davidson in his book *Radiation* (page 47) writes: 'subtle energy is the "ghost"-energy from which physical matter is derived'. He goes on to say: 'In our environment, the harmony or disharmony within subtle energy and the sub-atomic energy patterns, gives rise to the experience of good or bad atmospheres or vibrations . . . the disharmonizing of energy fields can . . . take place from within-out, as well as from without-in.'

In the West, when we refer to a person having energy we mean that they are vigorous and active; we are referring to a physical characteristic. In physics the term energy has a specific meaning: the capacity to do work. Work also has a specific meaning: it is what is done when a force moves – when work is done on an object, the object gains energy and the source of the work loses energy. Energy exists in many different forms, and it can change from one form to another; for example, food is an energy source which is changed into physical energy within the body. The subtle energy we are talking about here does not *move* anything in an obvious manner. However, as with physical energies it changes the state of the object of the work. David Spangler feels that subtle energies change how something is organized or how it organizes itself. He sees the subtle energy as replicating itself, for good or ill, within the object:

> Putting it simplistically, whereas physical energies in some manner move their object, subtle energies impregnate through resonance . . . How successfully they may do so depends on the clarity, strength and characteristics of . . . [the object's] inner identity, since it is by resonance that the induction takes place.[18]

CH'I AND THE ACUPUNCTURE MERIDIANS

The concept of the individual having an energy system is well established in Chinese medicine – and acupuncture meridians illustrate one aspect of this. In Chinese medicine, and many of the alternative and complementary therapies now becoming increasingly popular, the basic concept is that people's health and susceptibility to disease are determined by the health of their subtle energy system – and any damage to it will ultimately result in damage to the physical body.

This subtle energy system is partially based on the meridians. There are 14 major meridians, running skin deep over the head, torso and limbs. The meridians are bilateral, running as mirror images on both sides of the body. A beneficial form of subtle energy is absorbed by the body and is distributed throughout the body through the meridians. This energy is known as Ch'i (also spelt Chi) in traditional Chinese thought; in Hindu terminology it is called prana, and most Western writers refer to it as life force or vital force. Ch'i energy is seen as the basis of the life force; it is intrinsic within the universe and without it there could be no life. In his book *Vibrational Medicine*, Richard Gerber writes that 'this peculiar type of environmental subtle energy may have partial origin in solar radiation outside the recognised electromagnetic window of visible light' (page 176).

Dr Julian Kenyon has described various types of apparatus used to measure different aspects of the subtle energy system.[19] From this he concludes that Ch'i is 'related to electrical energy but there are other aspects of Ch'i which do not seem to relate to electromagnetism as we understand it at the present time'. We are not aware of Ch'i itself, because the energy is so perfectly balanced. Ch'i energy has been likened to an isometric exercise where two equal forces opposing each other give the impression of nothing happening. Neither are we aware of the mechanisms by which we absorb it. Some Ch'i energy is absorbed from physical substances – the air, water, food and sunlight – but more is absorbed directly from the universal supply of this energy.

Part of the role of Ch'i within the body seems to be to provide information to cells and between cells, over and beyond the information supplied through the nerves and the hormone system. Disease, then, is a sign that the flow of Ch'i is in some way faulty or unbalanced. The meridians are electromagnetic in nature and so are vulnerable to disturbance by other electromagnetic energies. Because the meridians are the channels or pathways through which the Ch'i energy flows into the physical tissues, their correct functioning is of vital importance to health.

The meridians form part of the interface between the physical and etheric bodies (see next section). Acupuncture points lie along these meridians and it is these which are needled during

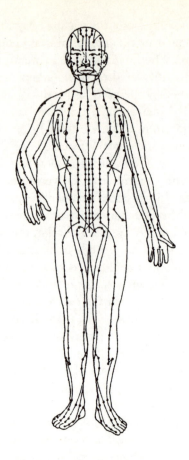

Figure 5 Diagram of acupuncture meridians

acupuncture treatment (*see figure 5*). The aim of this is to balance the flow of energy within the meridians. Skilled practitioners can 'feel' the location of these points. For a long time the power of acupuncture was dismissed by Western medicine because acupuncture theory did not fit with the medical understanding of how the body functions. However, gradually some doctors began to find that acupuncture could work for pain relief. As the body of evidence for the success of acupuncture with adults, babies and animals mounted, medical researchers began to consider more carefully subtle energy concepts such as meridians. In fact, the reality of meridians and acupuncture points is now beginning to be documented using radioactive tracer isotopes and sensitive electronic equipment. This suggests that meridians have a real physical presence.

THE SUBTLE BODIES

Some of the subtle energies associated with the physical body are usually called bodies themselves. There is much argument about how many subtle bodies there are and what they are called. Most writers on this subject accept that as well as a physical body, there is also an etheric body, an astral or emotional body, one or more mental bodies, and a spiritual body (see *figure 6*). Many systems of thought also include other additional bodies. The physical body is the material body that we can see, composed of atoms and molecules, obeying the laws of physics, chemistry and biology. The etheric body is seen to contain the blueprint for the physical body, determining how the foetus develops and how the body repairs itself when damaged. As the embryo develops, the single original cell divides and replicates itself many times. In some way, not yet fully understood by science, these cells eventually become specialist cells with a specific function in a particular part of the body. Richard Gerber in *Vibrational Medicine* (page 51) writes:

> This field or 'etheric body' is a holographic energy template that carries coded information to the spatial organization of the foetus as well as a roadmap for cellular repair in the event of damage to the developing organism.

The emotional body is the centre for emotions and feelings and it is here that the atmosphere around people is generated. The mental body (or bodies) is the source of thought: practical day-to-day thought, abstract philosophical thought and imagination. The spiritual body contains the sense of the divine. Many diagrams of subtle bodies show the higher bodies surrounding the lower bodies, but this is probably far from the truth. All the

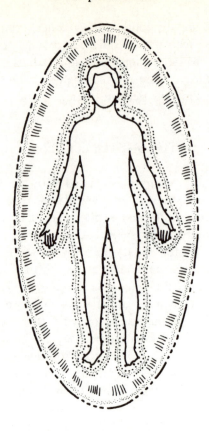

Figure 6 A representation of the subtle bodies

bodies interpenetrate each other and are interconnected in myriads of different ways, which are difficult to show in a diagram. They should be viewed much more as an interconnecting web than as layers in an onion or separate entities. Each subtle body is seen as having its own vibrational rate. The physical body can be seen precisely because it has a low vibrational rate, whereas the spiritual body cannot be seen because its vibrational rate is so high. The terms 'higher' and 'lower' are often used for these bodies, with the physical being the lowest and the spiritual the highest. This is unfortunate terminology, because it suggests that the physical body is in some way inferior to the others.

Subtle bodies have a being which is beyond the physical. It is hardly surprising that science has not identified these other bodies, because it is very much concerned with the material world. Belief in subtle bodies is not an attack on the scientific mode of enquiry; it merely suggests that the tools of scientific enquiry are not yet suitable for analysing and measuring these phenomena.

The Chakras

Although the individual subtle bodies have different vibrational rates, they have to be connected in some way. This is one of the functions of the chakras. In Sanskrit chakra means 'disc' or 'wheel', which is how they usually appear to clairvoyants. They are usually portrayed as energy vortices. Most writers in this field suggest that there are seven major chakras: the base chakra, the abdominal chakra, the solar plexus chakra, the heart chakra, the throat chakra, the brow or third eye chakra and the crown chakra. These are shown in *figure 7*. Each chakra is seen as having particular characteristics associated with it (for example, emotional qualities, colour or sound). Each chakra is also linked to a particular organ of the endocrine system. The throat chakra, for instance, is related to the thyroid gland (located in the throat) and is associated with the emotions of shyness and paranoia. The brow chakra is associated with the pituitary gland (the master gland of the hormonal system) and the emotions of anger and rage. Chakras connect the different bodies and provide a mechanism whereby the vibrational frequencies of one body can be accepted by another (similar to the gear system in a car). The chakras are the equivalent of step-down transformers: they change energy from one form to another, thereby allowing interaction between the various subtle bodies. It is likely that the chakras can be also damaged by geopathic energies. If this is the case, then some of the essential energy connections between the different bodies may not occur, leading eventually to illness.

However, it is also possible that through these connections, negative energies from any source are able to have an impact

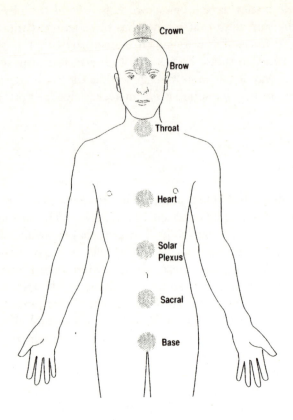

Figure 7 The seven chakras

and affect the health and well-being of people. These energies are not necessarily processed by the physical body, so their sphere of action cannot be judged in the physical realm alone. It may well be that some of these energies affect the subtle bodies. The physical body is then affected by its connection and interdependence on these other bodies for its overall health. This would explain the link between geopathic stress and cancer, where rogue cells continue to grow because the physical body seems to have lost its ability to destroy them. If we accept that part of the etheric body's role is to offer a controlling blueprint to the physical body, we need to be aware that this blueprint can be damaged by geopathic stress and so contain faulty information.

SUBTLE ENERGY HEALING

When the physical body is sick, healing can take place by working directly on the physical body, using, for instance, drugs or surgery. Alternatively, it is possible to work on one of the 'higher' bodies through energetic or vibrational medicine, leading through the chakras and meridians to an effect on the physical body. In a similar way, harm can also be inflicted on the physical body, directly by injury, accidents, bacteria and viruses, or through harm done to the 'higher' bodies. Most of the alternative therapies, such as kinesiology, acupuncture, homoeopathy and faith healing, employ subtle energy healing, correcting imbalances in the 'higher' bodies and the meridians, and then waiting for the concomitant change to happen in the physical body. Conventional medicine, on the other hand, is much more concerned with the physical body and, in its extreme form, sees man as only a complex machine.

Acupuncture, kinesiology (see page 68) and many other therapies work partly at the level of the acupuncture energy system to rebalance and control the flow of Ch'i energy within the body, bringing harmony and healing. When an acupuncturist puts needles into the body, he or she is directly influencing the flow of Ch'i within the meridian system by needling specific acupuncture points located along the meridians. These acupuncture points have been shown to have lower electrical resistance than the surrounding tissue. When a kinesiologist holds specific points on the physical body, he or she is rebalancing the meridian energy. For people who are used to Western medicine's intervention with surgery and potent drugs it is difficult to comprehend that anything can happen to a person's health as a result of this form of treatment. For others, conventional medicine with its focus on symptoms is often seen as hindering rather than healing the body. Alternative methods see symptoms and illness as indicators that all is not well at the subtle energy level. Nothing needs to be added, only adjustments made to what is already there. Medication or surgery solely to correct symptoms is seen as akin to shooting a messenger bringing bad news. It is felt that harmony will only return to the body when the energy system is rebalanced. Then the symptoms will disappear. We are probably all aware that certain emotions, such as excitement or fear, generate specific physical changes within the body. In a similar way, changes in the acupuncture energy system can affect the physical body, and damage to the physical body can affect the subtle energy system. It is a two-way process.

MORPHIC RESONANCE

Wider credence is now being given to the idea of some form of collective biological memory that does not follow normal rules. Rupert Sheldrake, a Cambridge biologist, calls this phenomenon 'morphic resonance'. It is very similar to the concept of subtle bodies found in many cultures and belief systems. Both involve something 'beyond the physical'. Morphic resonance attempts to explain why, after one generation of rats has learnt a trick, succeeding generations in other places seem to learn it more quickly. And why, once one bluetit had learnt to get milk out of a bottle by pecking through the foil top, suddenly bluetits all over England were doing the same thing. A new bluetit skill had appeared, even though there had been no obvious means of passing on this information. This phenomenon does not only apply to bluetits: people too seem to have similar abilities. The original theory, published in 1981, was greeted with scepticism and hostility by much of the scientific community. Yet the theory spawned a series of interesting experiments to test the hypothesis. The 1987 edition of *A New Science of Life* has a section describing some of the experiments that produced statistically significant results supporting the hypothesis. Further experiments have continued. The Institute of Noetic Studies in California arranged a competition to study this phenomenon. In one experiment people were shown groups of letters on a computer screen and asked to learn them. The results showed that once sequences had been learnt by one group of people they were easier for a subsequent group to learn. One of the award-winning entries was carried out in Nottingham, England. Students were asked to do four crossword puzzles: two that had been previously published in a London newspaper, and two that were awaiting publication. Although the students had not seen any of the crosswords before, they found it easier to complete the ones that had been previously published. In these experiments it seems that somehow the benefit of a prior experience can be passed on. Such a mechanism would make sense in terms of the survival of a species. If the benefits of learning and completing a task could be felt beyond the individual learning them, the skills of the whole species would improve, as would its ability to survive and prosper.

Sheldrake developed the idea of morphic resonance to solve the problem of how an egg grows into a chicken. He postulated a non-physical blueprint that contained the necessary information. This would also explain how, when a wound heals, the process of repair is turned off at just the right point so that the new skin is level with the surrounding areas. Sheldrake argued that these blueprints would be affected by previous generations of the species and so there would be a connection between generations through time and space. If this theory is correct, this would give rise to a mechanism through which various members of a species could communicate with each other without involving the normal physical senses. Obviously this communication would not be on a conscious level.

The 'proof' for morphic resonance and subtle bodies is to be found in their effect on the physical world, even though these concepts are not capable of being proved with physical-world tools. This would be like asking someone to use their eyes to detect smells, which is not possible because smells are not available to the receptors in the eyes. This does not mean that smells do not exist, only that our detection tool, the eye, is unsuitable for this particular job.

A LINKING FORCE?

All these phenomena suggest that there is something filling the space between physical bodies, or, at the very least, that connections can be made across this emptiness and some sort of 'energy' experienced. David Tansley in *Radionics Interface with the Ether Fields* referred to this as 'the formative matrix' and the 'energy field giving birth to matter'.[20]

In her book *Hands of Light*, Barbara Ann Brennan, a clairvoyant, writes (page 5):

> I discovered that everything has an energy field around it that looks somewhat like the light from a candle. I also began to notice that everything was connected by these energy fields, that no space existed without an energy field. Everything, including me, was living in a sea of energy.

Most people feel that the gap between objects is empty or composed solely of air. However, think about the effect some people can have on you when they enter a room. Sometimes their presence and energy (for good or ill) goes before them; you are aware of them even before you see them. And think how the energy of hyperactive children often fills a room. Their presence is much greater than their physical body. We have all had the feeling that someone is looking at us and turned to find that this is indeed true. Although we have not seen them, their concentration on us causes us to turn round. It is difficult to say what part of us does this sensing, but these instances show that we do sense something beyond physical bodies and beyond what our 'normal' senses can process. Similarly, most of us have had the experience of thinking about someone, or deciding to ring a particular person, only to have a phone call immediately from that same person. We often put these events down to coincidence, but the very least that can be said is that it is a frequent coincidence! There seems to be some link between us and other people, particularly those we love and care about.

This linking force may be the life principle which is in some ways common to all living beings. In different traditions this has different names: life force, Ch'i, vital energy, prana. All of these concepts suggest some linking between people, and some of them also suggest a linking between people and inanimate objects. Even some physicists now accept that much subatomic particle behaviour can only be explained by some, as yet unknown, linking force.

6

Detecting Geopathic Stress

Although some people may be aware that a place does not feel right, most people would not suspect geopathic stress. Sometimes there may be only a general feeling of unease and dissatisfaction, but if there are more definite health problems, and especially if they do not respond to treatment, it is worth checking the site for geopathic stress problems. If the sick person also has difficulty sleeping or has not been well since moving to a particular house, factory or office, this would further confirm the possibility of the presence of geopathic energies. If a woman has repeated miscarriages, this too may point in this direction. Having decided that it is worth investigating the possibility that geopathic problems are involved in a particular case of ill health, there are several options as to how to proceed.

DIY DETECTION

Although many people immediately want to consult an expert in this field, some people can, with a little thought and ingenuity, begin to develop some ability to detect these energies themselves. Once introduced to the concept of geopathic stress, many people find that they have some sense about the geopathic energies in their house. If they spend some time thoughtfully going around the house they will often sense in some undefined way where the best place is and, perhaps more importantly, where the worst place is. Persistent damp can be an indication of the presence of geopathic energies. Obviously a lot of damp exists because of poor ventilation, leaking roofs and so on, but if all the obvious structural faults have been corrected and damp still persists, it may well be worth looking at the possibility of a geopathic energy involvement. Many people's pulse rate will increase significantly when they spend some time in a geopathic area and this can be a useful guide.

Animal Behaviour

Observing the behaviour of animals can reinforce information gained in other ways. As mentioned earlier, there is a lot of anecdotal evidence that bees and ants flourish over energy lines that are detrimental to human beings, and that cats also like energy lines that are harmful for us. A surprisingly large number of the houses I have seen with a high degree of geopathic stress also contained cats that had once been strays. Often the owners recounted that they had not encouraged the cat to stay; some even actively discouraged it, but nevertheless the cat had persisted until it was accepted. It may well be that those cats chose the house because of its negative earth energies – but for them they were clearly positive rather than negative!

Sometimes a family pet will choose a particular spot to sleep even though there appear to be many more favourable places. Instead of sleeping in a sunny, cosy spot a cat may choose an awkward, draughty place with evident relish. These preferences could be indications of the presence of certain earth energies.

Plants

Plants can also give clues to the presence of lines of negative energies. Trees in particular will often appear to lean away from negative energies, although oaks, ash, willows, elder and elm benefit from being planted above these energies. In many parks, negative energy lines can be suspected just from looking at the way a whole series of trees grows in a particular direction without any obvious biological influence, such as the light or the direction of the wind. On one trip to Hyde Park in London a group of us traced such a negative energy line. When we continued it in our mind's eye into the distance we could see how the growth of the trees fitted with this line: trees were growing away from the line, even though they were in the middle of the park and in full light. Some of the trees also showed diseased nodules. Christopher Bird in *The Divining Hand* (page 270) recounts a study showing that on these lines apple trees develop cancerous growths, cherries show an abnormal increase in sap, and plum and pear trees rot or wither to death.

Even if the DIY approach does not reveal any indication of geopathic stress, it may still be appropriate to ask someone more experienced in these matters to check whether detrimental earth energies are involved in the problem.

OTHER DETECTION STRATEGIES

There are three ways of confirming the presence of geopathic stress: some people dowse (using rods or pendulums) for negative earth energies, others use kinesiology (or muscle testing as it is often known) to track these energies, and some individuals can 'see' or 'sense' them. Possibly we all have a latent ability to do this, but most of us have lost our connection with it. All of these strategies seem to use what Aubrey Westlake, in his foreword to David Tansley's book, called our 'supersensible sense'.[20] Dowsers and kinesiologists utilize this sense in a positive attempt to help people. They can communicate with the client on a level beyond that of normal communication, and the dowsing rods, the pendulum or the client's muscles become ways of manifesting this communication for the normal senses to access and interpret.

Dowsing

Dowsing, sometimes called divining, is an ancient art which is now enjoying a revival. Depictions of people dowsing have been found on Egyptian murals and ancient Chinese statues, but the real documentation of dowsing began with French priests in the 17th century. However, much of the knowledge about dowsing is not written down, but is passed on by experienced practitioners. Many have associated dowsing with the occult and devil-worshipping, so that those with the necessary skills often worked in secrecy or, at the very least, avoided negative publicity. Some people see dowsing as a suspicious activity, the interest of either fools or evil people. However, dowsing is now beginning to be viewed as a scientific tool, with the movement of the pendulum or rods being seen as an amplification of minute body movements – our vestigial rememberings of an ancient ability. It is now being used to detect water for farmers and water boards, and to detect minerals for exploration companies.

Dowsers often used pendulums when dealing with individual health problems or for assessing geopathic stress. The pendulum consists of a weight (usually made from wood or metal) suspended on the end of a string. The pendulum swings one way for 'yes' (usually clockwise) and another way for 'no', (usually anti-clockwise), but different people get different responses. The important thing when using a pendulum is that the response is consistent: a particular response from the pendulum always meaning 'yes' and another equally clear response always meaning 'no'. If dowsers are walking around a building or the countryside looking at geopathic problems they will often use rods (*figure 8*) as they are not overly influenced by the movement of walking. A pendulum used in this way will often sway with the motion of the body, so that any finer movement caused by changing geopathic energies is not so easily observed. Strong winds are a problem, even for the user of rods, as they can wobble in the wind, giving false readings. The rods can be made of metal, or sometimes a twig, traditionally hazel or willow, is used. One reason for using willow is that this tree is found near water. As the early dowsers were usually looking for water, they

Figure 8 Dowsing with rods

felt that willow had some affinity with it because of its preferred habitat. Rods can be made by cutting up a metal coat-hanger or they can be specially produced for the purpose. The rods or pendulum will exhibit some change when the person holding them is over an area that contains whatever is being actively looked for. Nevertheless, it is important to be precise about how to interpret this: is the negative energy under the dowser's feet or under his outstretched hands? Either could be correct, but it is important that the rods and pendulum are used in such a way that the location is always established in the same way.

Dowsers using a pendulum generally use a short pendulum or bob. The weight is suspended on a thin cord about 8 inches long. Some dowsers ask for the pendulum to swing in a particular way when they are standing over an area of geopathic stress. Some dowsers carry a 'witness' in their hands while doing this, while some pendulums have a space in the weight to house the witness. A witness is a sample of whatever the dowser is trying to find. Finding a sample is not a problem when the object of the search is water or a particular metal. However, it becomes more of a problem when the dowser is searching for geopathic energies. At the moment I am researching a set of energies that could be used for this purpose – in the form of small vials of liquid containing the homoeopathic imprint of each of the different energies.

Some dowsers use a long pendulum. Here the weight is attached to a much longer cord, often about 40 inches in length, which can be adjusted according to what is being sought. The most thorough work on this subject was done by T C Lethbridge. He found that his long pendulum gyrated in the presence of copper when the length of the cord was 30.5 inches, in the presence of iron when the cord was 32 inches, and so on. He also found that the pendulum would react to ideas. Interestingly, both silver and the moon caused a rotation of the pendulum at 30 inches, but the number of rotations would be different depending on which one he was thinking about. To the best of my knowledge no specific lengths are yet established for geopathic energies.

Christopher Bird in *The Divining Hand* explains how Dr Zaboj V Harvalik, a physicist and scientific advisor to the US Army's Advanced Material Concepts Agency, undertook to find out more about the ability to dowse. He conducted various tests and concluded that the organs in the body responsible for sensing these changes in the earth's energies were the adrenal glands and the pineal gland. The stimulus was then transmitted to the brain and back out to the muscles of the arms. He also concluded that almost anyone could be taught to dowse, although many people needed to drink some water before starting. He also found that many dowsers would activate rods in other people's hands simply by thinking 'exciting thoughts'.

There is no totally convincing explanation of *how* dowsing works, but there is more and more evidence that it *does* work. Most authorities agree with Harvalik that the dowser picks up minute variations in the earth's magnetic field. These variations cause minor changes in muscles, including those in the wrists. The rod or pendulum then makes these changes visible to the naked eye and thereby to the conscious attention of the dowser. A small change in muscle tension becomes a much larger change in the movement of the rod or pendulum. Having said this, when you dowse, it should *feel* as though the rods or pendulum are moving of their own accord, not being influenced by you. This, however, does not explain how many dowsers can work from maps. Both Harvalik and Tom Graves recognize that as yet there is no adequate explanation for how map dowsing works, but both believe that there is incontrovertible evidence that it does.

As Tom Graves points out in *The Dowser's Workbook* (page 11): 'Dowsing rarely makes sense in theory, but does work surprisingly well in practice if *you* let it work.' His excellent book takes you step by step through the procedure of learning how to dowse and also teaches you how to make a dowsing rod from two metal coat-hangers, and how to make a pendulum from a cotton reel or a used AA battery.

The British Society of Dowsers offers short courses in dowsing for anyone interested in learning this fascinating skill (see page 125 for details). The Society feels that most people can learn the art 'by practice and perseverance', although some people will have a more natural aptitude for it than others.

Kinesiology

Kinesiology also suffers from the derision of the sceptics. While dowsing uses rods or pendulums to amplify the body's response, kinesiology uses a person's muscle or muscles. Kinesiology utilizes the fact that when anything stresses the body it causes muscles to weaken. This is normally imperceptible, but in kinesiology muscles are tested in isolation (as far as possible) and small variations in muscle strength are evident. Kinesiology was developed by Dr George Goodheart, an American chiropractor, in 1964. There is another discipline called kinesiology, used by physiotherapists and others, which is concerned with the mechanics of movement and the physiological state of the muscles themselves. Kinesiology as developed by Dr Goodheart went beyond this, using the muscle response as an indicator of other aspects of the body's functioning. He discovered that testing a muscle for muscle strength reveals other things about the body. For instance, it can be related to the acupuncture system. Kinesiology developed using some of the insights of chiropractic coupled with Chinese acupuncture knowledge. Very quickly it was found that muscle testing could be used for many things other than structural work on the body.

Kinesiology has continued to develop and now there are various approaches, such as Health Kinesiology, Applied Kinesiology and Clinical Kinesiology, each one using the basic technique of muscle testing in a slightly different system. All of these different types of kinesiology look at the whole body and offer a synthesis of some of the insights of acupuncture with structural, nutritional assessment and so on. Kinesiology can be used to help people deal with emotional stress, to help counteract physical symptoms such as arthritis, eczema and migraine, and to improve memory and correct dyslexia. It can also be used to help people achieve their potential in sport, the creative arts and any other aspect of their lives. It can also be used to assess and correct geopathic stress. Treatment involves using acupuncture points and reflex areas on the body to correct imbalances and energy blocks, so allowing the body to regain its balance and wholeness. Some kinesiologists, particularly those practising Health Kinesiology, are trained to help people be less susceptible to any geopathic energies they encounter. Kinesiology offers a form of treatment that is uniquely tailored to the individual, as determined by the muscle testing. This means that no two consultations or treatments are identical, even where people have the same symptoms.

In kinesiology a muscle response is used for assessment. In order for this to be accurate it is necessary to make sure that the person's acupuncture energy system is balanced. Different kinesiologies have different pre-checks and ways of attaining this balance, but with all systems the initial aim is to ensure that the acupuncture energies are flowing in a balanced manner.

Figure 9 Muscle testing

Only then can muscle testing begin, usually on one of the arm muscles. The person being tested holds one arm out straight, either in front or to the side, at an angle of between 45 and 90 degrees (see *figure* 9). This is designed, in as far as it is possible, to isolate the muscle (usually the anterior deltoid or the middle deltoid) so that any weakness of functioning becomes easily evident. With the subject keeping the arm in this position, the tester stands facing the subject and applies gentle downward pressure on the arm just above the wrist as he or she asks questions. The person being tested attempts to anchor the arm in the initial position. Under this pressure the arm either locks in position (a positive or 'yes' response) or gives way (a negative or 'no' response). This is not a form of arm wrestling or a test of how strong a person is, but a sensitive test of the muscle response to different stimuli. Both people should use the same amount of pressure each time. Obviously there will be slight variations in the amount of pressure used, but these are within the tolerance for the test when performed by a skilled operator. Different muscles are related to different aspects of the body's functioning. For example, testing the anterior deltoid muscle in this way can tell us about the gall bladder meridian, whereas testing the quadriceps gives us information about the small intestine meridian. In Health Kinesiology, and some other kinesiologies, only one muscle is chosen and is used as an indicator of stresses and problems throughout the whole energy system.

Clients experiencing their first kinesiology session will often ask: 'Who is responding? Who is answering your questions? It can't be *me*, because I often do not even understand the nature of the question, let alone what the answer should be.' Obviously, the tester is not asking the conscious mind. If this were the case, it would be much simpler to just ask the question and wait for the person's verbal response. A limited explanation is that the kinesiologist is asking the body's maintenance system about itself. This maintenance system is called the homoeostatic mechanism; it is the body's ability to maintain its own internal environment in the face of a changing external environment. For example, the external temperature can vary enormously, but the body maintains its own internal temperature within very narrow limits. If we are in a hot environment we sweat in order to cool the skin through evaporation. In a cold environment we shiver and the hair on our body stands on end. We do not have to make conscious decisions to do this, because, fortunately, it is all taken care of by the homoeostatic system within the body. At any time our bodies have to know what our blood pressure is and what our temperature is. They do not know this in terms of conventional medicine. They cannot tell us that out blood pressure is 140/80, for example. However, they do know if it is too high or too low, and through the homoeostatic mechanism attempt to correct it. In kinesiology, this information that the body has about itself is, at least partly, being accessed. Questions are asked and the response is amplified through the muscle reaction of the testing, so that the answer can be 'read'. It is interesting that the body's response is a binary system, involving two possibilities, 'yes' and 'no'. In a similar way, the homoeostatic mechanism within the body, which is concerned with maintaining balance, has two responses, 'too much' and 'not enough'.

Anyone wishing to learn more about kinesiology should contact The Kinesiology Federation for the name of a local practitioner or teacher. The Federation represents people from all the different branches of kinesiology. Anyone specifically interested in learning Health Kinesiology or finding a practitioner should contact the author. For further details and Useful Addresses see page 123.

Many dowsers and kinesiologists can offer help in correcting geopathic disturbances in homes and work places. But it is not sufficient to ascertain that a problem exists; the exact method for correcting it is important too.

It cannot be emphasized enough that both dowsing and kinesiology are 'operator sensitive', that is, they are very dependent on the skills of the practitioner for the accuracy and validity of the results. In addition, not all kinesiologists or dowsers have an interest in the problems of geopathic stress. If you decide to consult one of these people for this reason you need to make certain that they have a particular interest and aptitude in this field.

Certainly the evidence from both practices suggests that the person carrying out the dowsing or the kinesiology is making the result happen. The pendulum, the rods and the subject's arm amplify small muscle changes. In the case of dowsing these muscle changes come from the arm of the person doing the testing. In the case of kinesiology it would appear that they can come from either the tester or the subject, or both. So when critics say that the person is moving the rods, the pendulum or the arm, this is in fact true. However, what they usually mean by this is that the operator is behaving dishonestly and performing some hoax. Reputable practitioners of dowsing and kinesiology strive to avoid influencing the results, so that the response is an amplification of unconscious changes in muscle response, rather than a conscious effort to make something happen. Kinesiology and dowsing may well be amplifying our psychic response, and changing it into a form which we can handle.

Sensing the Energies

When you talk to people who can 'see' or 'sense' these energies, they often find it difficult to explain how the process happens and what exactly it is that they see. They may say that the air appears less clear, less vibrant, or more dense in areas of geopathic stress. They may say some geopathic energies appear as smoke or spirals or black walls. Often they will say that it is not like normal seeing, but when pressed cannot explain how it is different. This is not very useful for anyone who may be trying to develop this skill. However, it does seem that many people can develop some level of ability if they work with these energies consistently using, say, kinesiology and dowsing. It may well be that we all have this latent ability.

Some people feel that dowsing and kinesiology are more objective than a straight psychic response. This is not true: the dowsing rod and muscle testing are as open to influence, intentional or unintentional, as the reaction of the person who 'sees' energies. Most practitioners act in good faith and with an open mind, but, unfortunately, some people unintentionally influence the results they find by believing strongly that they will find a particular type of energy at a particular site. Of course, it is necessary to have some model to work from, but it is important that this model is open to change and refutation.

It is important, however, that the person doing the testing has a clear understanding of what he or she is looking for. Some years ago a client asked me if I could help her find some gold sovereigns which were reputed to be in her house, hidden there by a long-dead sea captain. Using kinesiology I asked: 'Is there any hidden treasure in this house?' The response was positive, and so amid great excitement we tested to find the exact spot. Finally we came to the conclusion that the treasure was under a large chest freezer in the basement. When this was removed, hidden treasure was indeed found: a one pound coin which had obviously rolled under there at some point! She did dig down into the floor, but found nothing further. My question had been about hidden treasure, not about gold sovereigns. This story highlights how important it is to be clear about what you are asking. I should, of course, have asked the question: 'Are there any gold sovereigns buried in this house?' The adage about computers, 'garbage in, garbage out', holds true for kinesiology testing and dowsing as well.

Whatever energy-detecting method is chosen, the first stage is

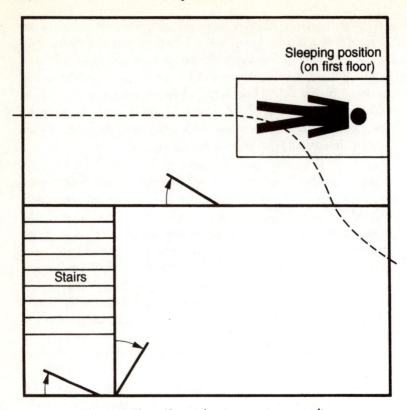

Figure 10 Plan of house showing negative energy line

to walk around the site and develop some sort of 'feel' for the place. The practitioner will then start to test the area, moving in a systematic way in order to cover the whole site. While doing this, it is necessary to keep in mind all the different types of energy. As well as looking for negative energy lines, such as black lines, it is important to look for spirals and clouds. It is also important to remember that not all geopathic phenomena are found at ground level. Energy drains, for example, can be located in mid-air. The findings are usually noted on a plan. Most practitioners develop different symbols for different types of energy. Particular attention needs to be paid to the area directly below any beds or favourite chairs. Some practitioners like to work with a scale for geopathic stress. For instance, zero would indicate a complete absence of any form of geopathic stress and 100 would mean it is impossible to add any geopathic stress to make the situation worse: the area is geopathically saturated. Often they will wish to ascertain the worst and the best spot on the site. *Figure 10* shows a typical house with the negative energies marked.

Working directly with geopathic energies in this way can be very draining, so many practitioners move away from the site for short rests, returning when they feel able to. I myself find that if I spend too long examining a site I become disorientated and develop low back pain. For this reason some people feel more comfortable working with a plan of the site. In general, a kinesiologist working with a plan in this way would still wish, if possible, to muscle test someone who lives or works at the site, or to have made a prior visit to the site.

Having established that there is a problem with geopathic energies, the next step is to work out how to fix them. If all else fails it is possible to move from a home or work place, but for most people a more practical option is to correct the area in question.

7

Correcting Geopathic Stress

Correcting geopathic disturbances is not always difficult and complicated, although sometimes it can be. The first and simplest solution is to try moving the bed or desk to another place. Sometimes people's health and well-being improves dramatically from this one simple measure. Kathe Bachler's book *Earth Radiation* lists many cases where doing just this has produced spectacular results. This is partly because we spend such a large part of the day in bed, and partly because if the bed is over detrimental earth energies, sleep is unlikely to be refreshing and healing. It is ironic that many sick people spend a lot of time in bed, unaware that often, at least part of the reason for their ill health is because the bed is in a geopathically stressed area. Unfortunately it is possible that the bed will be moved from one harmful area to another. It is surprising, though, how many people can instinctively find a good place for themselves once they know about the problem of geopathic stress. Many small babies seem intuitively to move away from negative energy lines. If a baby is observed always sleeping to one end of its cot it would probably indicate that the cot should be moved in that direction so that the baby can sleep more peacefully.

As was explained in the previous chapter, it is good to be guided by any animals in the house. At the very least I would not advise having beds directly above or below or on an area

Correcting Geopathic Stress

where a cat likes to sleep. A spot favoured by a dog will, in general, be a good place to put a bed or a desk.

If moving the bed or desk does not lead to an improvement in health, do not immediately assume that the problem is not geopathic stress. Sometimes there appears to be no really satisfactory space within the house or work place and remedial action will need to be taken. However, the results are usually well worth the effort and money.

Obviously, when testing for geopathic energies, each situation is unique. It may well be that there are many underlying rules about both the detection and treatment of these energies, but as yet we know but few of them. Each situation demands a different solution, depending on the exact configuration of energies present. Often a skilled dowser or kinesiologist needs to be involved to decide, firstly, what the problem is, and secondly, how it can be corrected. It is not, as yet, possible to give rules about how particular energies can be fixed. We have already seen that there are many different types, each with its own characteristics and origins. Because of this it is not possible to correct all energies in the same way. Some people involved in this field do claim with sincerity to be able to do this, either by using some patented device or by psychically re-routing the negative energies. It seems that they are usually correcting only a limited number of disturbed energies (often ley lines or underground water problems) and are unaware of other energies that may also need attention.

An additional consideration is that some techniques which appear to correct geopathic stress may simply mask the problem and the negative energy will continue to do harm. This is particularly dangerous because it lulls people into a false belief that an area is now safe. They may respond for a while and then the old symptoms of ill health will return. In this case it is likely that the initial response is a placebo reaction, and with time the harm from the geopathic energies will become obvious again.

Geopathic energies can be handled in several different ways: they can be reflected or refracted, absorbed, blocked or transformed. Different types of energies need to be corrected in different ways. In one case, reflecting an energy may be appropriate, in another it may be appropriate to block it. It is vitally important, however, that whatever method is used, the undesirable energies are not reflected to affect someone else.

Different materials have different properties in relation to geopathic energies. Aluminium, graphite, quartz, elder and elm, for instance, can block the flow of energy when placed correctly. Lethbridge called these energy interrupters. On the other hand, mirrors, when properly sited, can reflect negative energies away from a building. These different characteristics are not surprising when we consider how materials have distinct properties in relation to electricity and magnetism. For example, water is a good conductor of electricity, as is copper, whereas wood, rubber, glass and plastic are poor conductors. Similarly plastic, wood, glass, copper and aluminium cannot be magnetized, whereas iron, steel and nickel can. If geopathic stress is indeed an electromagnetic phenomenon, a substance's ability to become magnetized or to conduct electricity will be relevant when choosing material to counteract it. This is analogous to the different methods of stopping radiation, another part of the electromagnetic spectrum. Beta waves can be stopped by aluminium, whereas x-rays and gamma rays will pass through it. X-rays can be stopped by lead, but it takes thick concrete to stop gamma rays. The effect of all three different types of radiation is the same – damage to living tissues – but the method of stopping them is different. Each type of geopathic stress may exert the same damaging effect on an organism, but will need to be corrected in a different way. It is very quickly apparent if you work with these energies that one method of correcting them is not suitable for all situations.

CORRECTIVE DEVICES

The various artefacts used for correcting geopathic stress are not necessarily placed directly over any negative energy line or spot. The exact positioning has to be established by careful testing using kinesiology or dowsing. Often several different objects will work in conjunction with each other, correcting the negative energy of the site, but sometimes each negative energy will have to be corrected by a specific and different type of object. In checking what is to be done it is important to bear both these possibilities in mind.

Crystals

Crystals are probably used more frequently than anything else. Expensive, beautiful crystals can be used but, fortunately, this is not necessary. Crushed marble, which can be bought from some garden centres or from a monument maker, will do the job perfectly well at a fraction of the cost of quartz or amethyst crystal. Crystals, particularly quartz, are seen as having special energy properties. Quartz is used in electronic watches because it vibrates at a steady pace with little generation of heat, and so can be used to measure time accurately. Healers also consider that crystals have other properties and can focus healing energies from one individual to another. In *Vibrational Medicine* Gerber writes that quartz crystals will vibrate at different rates depending on what energy is put into the crystal, so that pressure would result in a different vibration from sound. It would seem likely that the crystal is in some way changing the frequency of the geopathic energies to one that is more acceptable to the humans exposed to it. It has also been suggested that crystals 'absorb' geopathic energies. The amount of crystals necessary (in weight) is determined by testing as is the location or locations. Frequently the crystals need to be placed in several different places. Regardless of what type is used, it is important to wash the crystals regularly to remove any accumulation of negative energy. The simplest way to do this is to place them in a bucket and run water over them for about half an hour. How often this should be done, and the exact length of time for the cleaning process, can be established by kinesiology or dowsing.

After attending a workshop I taught on geopathic stress, a consulting engineer subsequently checked a stable for these energies. The owner was particularly concerned because one of the horses was unpredictable and vicious. As this was a riding school with a large clientele of small children, the owner was considering having the horse put down. The engineer checked the stables and advised that two piles of crystals (10lbs in all) should be put in the stables at strategic spots. The owner was delighted to find that the horse's temper improved to such an extent that she was able to abandon any thought of having it put down. She also found that other horses had been affected. One mare, who had been particularly difficult to get into her box, now went in without any problem. All the horses and ponies were generally less skittish in the yard once the GS had been corrected.

Coils

Coils are usually used in pairs, one with a clockwise rotation and one anticlockwise. They are made from ten revolutions of thick copper wire, with a spike sticking up at an angle of 45 degrees. The length of the spike and the diameter of the coil need to be the same. Although they need to be accessible, the coils should be placed as high as possible in a house; perhaps hung from a ceiling or placed in the loft. They appear to accumulate negative energy by trapping it within the coils, and for this reason they need to be washed in the same way as crystals. Excellent coils made for this purpose can be purchased from Mr E Borrelli (see Useful Addresses section). *Figure 11* shows the house we saw in the previous chapter, but this time remedial action, using a combination of crystals and coils, has been marked in as well.

Mirrors

Mirrors will reflect negative energy in the same way as they reflect light. As it is thought that the mirror reflects the negative ray back onto itself, thereby cancelling out the charge, the size and exact placing of the mirrors are important. Most people, of course, have mirrors in their houses for other reasons. However, all mirrors can have an effect on geopathic energies, depending

Correcting Geopathic Stress

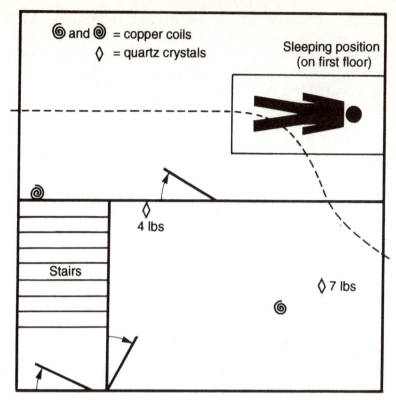

Figure 11 Plan of house showing corrective measures

on their placing, so it may be necessary to take down a mirror or move it to another place as part of the solution to these energy problems.

My easiest geopathic case of all was a simple matter of moving a mirror. The client had been experiencing stomach problems for some time. Initially I did not suspect geopathic stress, as we had previously checked her house and corrected the problem. Eventually, after drawing a blank on other possibilities, I decided to check the house again. Through kinesiology testing I learnt that the stomach problem *was* related to geopathic stress. I checked my previous assessment and correction methods and found that something had subsequently changed. When I checked a plan of the house I found a mirror was indicated in the client's bedroom. She looked surprised and told me that there was a wardrobe on that wall and one of its sliding doors was mirrored. By sliding the doors the other way the mirror was then in the correct place to neutralize the geopathic energy. She then remembered that she used to have the wardrobe doors in this position, but some months previously had changed them over. This had coincided with the onset of her stomach symptoms. Once the doors were changed over, her stomach problems disappeared. The client was amazed and thrilled at this simple solution to her problems.

Aluminium Foil

Aluminium foil is sometimes used to correct negative energy. Normal aluminium foil bought for cooking will usually be adequate, but it is advisable to use several layers for robustness and to overlap any joins. It is necessary to check the foil regularly to make sure it has not been punctured, thereby allowing energy to leak through. If it has, the area can be patched, or the whole foil replaced.

One of my clients, a boy of 12, had problems with allergies. He was prone to headaches and recurring earache. He was also allergic to swimming pool water. On testing him I found that his lymph system needed strengthening, which I did using Health Kinesiology techniques. Initially there was some improvement in his health, but as this did not continue I began to suspect geopathic problems. When I tested his house I did indeed find them. Further testing indicated that the solution was to fasten a piece of aluminium foil 3 feet by 3 feet at a carefully tested place on one inside wall of the house. The parents were, not surprisingly, sceptical, but willing to do this and see what happened. They were delighted when their son's health problems disappeared.

Occasionally it is possible for either foil or a mirror to be used, but sometimes it has to be one or the other. This can be established by careful and accurate kinesiology testing or dowsing. Usually it is not necessary for either foil or mirrors to be exposed, so they can, if convenient, be hidden by furniture. Both can be covered with wallpaper or paint, if practicable, without this affecting their function. When using foil or mirrors the exact size has to be established. Sometimes the measurements are precise, sometimes expressed in terms of minimums and maximums. Also, the exact positioning is crucial. As well as establishing which wall or walls are involved, the height above the floor and the position of the edges from the corners of the room need to be checked carefully.

Metal Plates

Metal plates, often made of galvanized steel, are sometimes placed on the floor of a building. They are often used in pairs orientated at right angles. Once again, the exact dimensions and placing are critically important, but an average plate would measure 3-4 feet wide and 6-8 feet long. Fortunately, as the plates do not usually need to be on view, they can be covered with tiles, carpet or rugs.

Cosmic Batteries

Cosmic batteries were developed by a Belgian dowser for use in radionics. They comprise a series of 34 glass tubes containing numbers, metal coils, homoeopathic remedies and so on, in a precise configuration. Each tube serves a different purpose. Some of these are designed specifically for correcting a range of environmental energy problems.

Rods

Rods used for correcting geopathic problems are usually copper or iron and have to be solid, usually at least half an inch in diameter. Considerable effort may have to be expended to put the rods in exactly the right place. I once instructed some of my clients to put a series of rods approximately 1 foot away from an outer wall of their house. I used kinesiology to establish the exact length of the rods, and the owners of the house were amazed that the rods went into the ground just the right amount before a change in rock strata would have made further penetration difficult. Presumably the rods had to be this specific length to counteract the change in rock strata, but none of us had prior knowledge of this change in the geology. Usually, rods have to be hammered in so that their tops are about 6 inches below the level of the ground. In one case it became evident that it was important to keep the space between the top of the rod and ground level clear of debris, otherwise the benefit of the rods would have been severely diminished. Often a series of rods is placed along one side of a house, at an equal distance apart. Some dowsers claim to be able to change the direction of underground water streams by hammering rods into the ground at appropriate points.

Colour

Colour can be used in many ways. Sometimes a wall needs to be painted a particular colour or a coloured light bulb needs to be placed in a particular spot. The colour of light is related to the wavelength of the light waves. For instance, red has a longer wavelength than violet. Because of this, different colours have different energy properties, which can be used to alter geopathic energies. The precise colour and location have to be determined by testing.

Magnets

Magnets are sometimes used to correct energy disturbances. They are often placed on incoming water pipes and power lines. Often between two and four magnets are placed on the pipe with their south-seeking poles pointing inwards. Usually the magnets need to be 800-1,200 gauss in strength, and magnetized so there is only one pole on each face. When the magnet is used in this way it seems to induce all the electrons to flow and spin in the same direction, thus making them less of a problem for susceptible individuals. Magnets can also be placed on walls, ceilings or floors to counteract geopathic problems. Traditional school magnets are magnetized through the ends, and the magnetic strip used on doors is magnetized across the width but with alternating poles. Neither of these types is suitable and it will be necessary to obtain one from a specialist magnet company (see Useful Addresses section).

Apopi Spheres

Apopi spheres are made of plastic and are about 3.5cm (1½ inches) in diameter. They are said to contain 'specific combinations of metals or metalloids' that cannot be produced by the human body but can be found in trace amounts in plants. These micro-element minerals are held in a pure water solution in very low concentrations. In many ways their action is akin to that of homoeopathic remedies. There are ten different types of Apopi spheres, each containing a different combination of micro-elements, kept secret by the inventor, Charles Beijns. The micro-elements are also designed to be taken internally to assist in the treatment of a wide range of health problems. Each type of sphere is designed to neutralize specific geopathic or electromagnetic phenomena. The unassuming appearance of these plastic balls belies their power. In A *New Energetic Technology* (page 10), Charles Beijns describes the action of these spheres in the following way:

> The APOPI appliances supply a positive energy alteration to our environment: it establishes the balance of the cosmic radiation by the transmission of frequencies higher than those of our organic living cells.

Apopi spheres are made by Arophar in Belgium and imported into the UK by Herbamin (see Useful Addresses section).

Shapes

Great care should be taken when using shapes, particularly pyramids. Pyramids can amplify energy, whether it is positive or negative. Obviously we would not want negative energy enhanced. Some shapes will block energy rather than enhancing it. Accurate testing will decide where the shape is to go, its size, and the materials for its construction.

Photographs

Sometimes an image of the building can be used, usually a black and white negative. The exact angle from which the photograph needs to be taken has to be carefully tested for, as does the place in which it is then buried. Sometimes the photograph needs to be buried with a mirror underneath it.

Plants

Certain plants are good indicators of the presence or absence of geopathic stress. Sometimes they are also used to correct GS, although this is not very common. However, there is already significant evidence that plants can be used to remove environmental pollutants. NASA conducted studies over 15 years on the use of plants, as they were interested in developing bioregenerating life-support systems for space stations. Some plants were found to be able to remove benzene, formaldehyde and trichloroethylene from the air on a sustainable basis. The scientific basis for using plants for geopathic purposes has yet to be established. If they are used, it is necessary to test for which type of plant to use and its placing. Sometimes several plants, either of the same or different types, will need to be used.

Symbols

Symbols, often drawn on card, can dramatically alter the feel and quality of both negative and positive energy. Any symbol

Figure 12a The 'Starburst' symbol

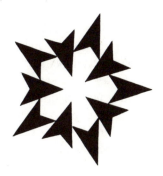

Figure 12b The 'Arrowheads' symbol

Figure 12c The 'Roundel' symbol

could be appropriate, but it would be necessary to establish the size and colours of both the symbol and the background card. The exact nature of the symbol and the positioning of it in the house are also important. All of the different factors involved can be established by careful questioning using dowsing or kinesiology. Recently I have been using a set of 12 symbols called Health Through The Eyes, designed by Heather Willings (see Useful Addresses section). Each of these cards strengthens a particular acupuncture meridian. Heather found the 12 symbols, whose exact colouring and proportions were determined, through dowsing. She was also guided by her intuition and meditation. The cards can clearly be used in several different ways. If a person has an imbalance in a particular meridian, looking at the relevant symbol for a while will rebalance the meridian. People are, in fact, often attracted to the very symbol they need and, given the choice, will choose the right card. Each card is also related to particular emotional qualities. The symbol named 'Starburst', for instance, (*figure 12a*) can correct imbalances in the stomach meridian and is also used for confidence, perseverance, acceptance of what is necessary, and the assurance to overcome adversity. It can also help free blocked energy and cleanse negative emotions. The 'Arrowheads' symbol (*figure 12b*) supports the kidney meridian and is also for decisiveness, tenacity, willpower and strength to assume responsibility. It is also said to harmonize physical and spiritual energy. The 'Roundel' (*figure 12c*) relates to the small intestine meridian and encourages cheerfulness, contentment, serenity, and a clear view of the present. It also helps to restore emotional energy and to improve relationships with other people. These 12 powerful symbols can also be used to counteract geopathic problems. Again it is necessary to find which symbol or symbols are to be used and their exact placing. Although the emotional qualities attached to the cards are often a useful indicator of which cards to use for healing purposes, they do not help when it comes to choosing the appropriate cards for correcting houses. It would then be necessary to test by kinesiology or dowsing. In some houses several of the same cards may be used, whereas in others it may be only one card or several different ones. Heather is currently working on cards to rebalance the chakras, and it may well be that these too are useful for correcting geopathic problems.

Ceremonies or Rituals

Ceremonies are sometimes appropriate for correcting geopathic energies. Many churches have a history of using them in connection with the paranormal, but it is possible to use ceremonies without any religious connotations at all. For some people the term ceremony or ritual implies some association with devil worship. Used in the context of geopathic work, they have absolutely no involvement with black magic.

Energy drains (discussed in Chapter 3) are corrected in this manner. The ceremony seems to restore them to their proper functioning. Often the ceremony is very simple – a common format involves a particular number of people holding hands in a circle and walking a specific number of times around the energy drain. Sometimes the people involved are asked to visualize something at the same time – in one case, a red poppy. Very often the sex of the people forming the circle is important. This method of energy correction is particularly interesting in the light of J Havelock Fidler's discussion of the dream he had of people dancing around a standing stone in order to charge it (*Ley Lines*, Chapter 5). The importance of the sex of the participants ties in with Lethbridge's work on energetically charged stones, where the sex of the charger is clearly transmitted to the stone.

Ceremonies are also used where stones have become inappropriately emotionally charged by the builder or previous occupant of a building. There is no standard format for these ceremonies. Common components include lighting candles, saying certain things in particular rooms, and specific visualizations. Sometimes it is important who is involved in the ceremony: it may have to be specific individuals, or the sex or age of the participants may be important.

Even when a building has been properly assessed and remedial action taken, it is important to monitor the situation from time to time. Geopathic stress can change over time for reasons that are not totally understood, although seasonal factors certainly play a part. In Canada, for example, it has been found that there can be significant differences in geopathic energies between winter and summer in areas where the ground freezes to a considerable depth in the winter. It has been suggested that the sunspot cycle may also be important. There are often more obvious reasons for changing or fluctuating geopathic situations. Alterations or even redecoration within a house can change the existing situation by, for instance, deflecting or concentrating harmful energies in different areas within the house. Building work in nearby houses and work places may cause problems in the same way.

8

Geopathic Stress and Feng Shui

Feng Shui, literally 'wind-water', is a centuries-old Chinese art which attempts to look at the flow of energies in the landscape and to integrate man, buildings and the landscape into a harmonious whole. Two of these energies are wind and water, hence the name. When balance and harmony are attained good health, happiness and prosperity will result. Feng Shui almost certainly grew out of the recognition that man tends to prosper in certain environments – where there is sunshine, but not too much heat; where there is rain and water, but not floods and damp. In other words man survives and prospers when there is some balance within the landscape and the climate.

Sarah Rossbach writes in *Feng Shui*:

> Despite its pragmatic aspect, feng shui is in a sense a rosetta stone linking man and his environment, ancient ways and modern life. It interprets the language articulated by natural forms and phenomena, by man-made buildings and symbols, and by the continual workings of the universe, including moon phases and star alignments. Feng shui is the key to understanding the silent dialogue between man and nature, whispered through a cosmic breath or spirit – ch'i. . . . If ch'i is misguided, man's life and luck might falter. Man feels and is affected by ch'i, though he may not know it.

Feng Shui experts believe that it is possible to influence how people feel and behave by influencing the environment in which they live. This is now accepted by modern Western architects, who recognize more and more that buildings should fit people and not the other way round. In Chinese culture, though, this idea has always been given much more weight. Feng Shui goes beyond looking at the physical arrangement of the environment and what is aesthetically pleasing.

CH'I

Central to Feng Shui is the concept of Ch'i. The Chinese geomancy expert looks at the environment in terms of energy, or Ch'i. Feng Shui practices are designed to heal the flow of Ch'i so that it moves freely without violence or stagnation. As we have already seen, Ch'i is the essential primary subtle energy of the universe, flowing into man and becoming his own personal Ch'i. The Feng Shui expert needs great understanding of this energy in order to make the best use of it. Sarah Rossbach (page 21 of *Feng Shui*) describes Ch'i as:

> . . . a life essence, a motivating force. It animates all things. Ch'i determines the height of mountains, the quality of blooms, the extent of potential fulfilment. Without ch'i, trees will not blossom, rivers will not flow, man will not be.

YIN AND YANG

In considering the harmonious flow of Ch'i, the Chinese draw on the concepts of yin and yang. Ch'i energy is both yin and yang. Yin is often depicted as female energy, whereas male energy is yang. Heaven is seen as male and the earth as female; what is between has to develop a balance between male and female so that harmony and balance can ensue. As well as being male, yang energy is seen as active, light and expansive, whereas yin energy is regarded as passive, dark and receptive (see *figure 13*). Too much 'male' energy is harmful, just as too much

Geopathic Stress and Feng Shui

Yang	Yin
Light	Dark
Sunny	Cloudy
Sun	Moon
Heaven	Earth
Day	Night
Fire	Water
Heat	Cold
Dryness	Dampness
Expansive	Receptive
Masculine	Feminine

Figure 13 The yin/yang symbol and some characteristics

'female' energy is. Harmony is achieved when yin and yang energy are in balance. Yin and yang are not seen as being in conflict: they depend on each other. This balance is not static, although it is often depicted in this way. It is a dynamic fluctuating balance leading to growth, change and harmony. A static balance would lead to rigidity and death without renewal. Life is seen as a continuous cycle of yang and yin. Death leads to new life, rest leads to renewal and new activity, night is followed by day, winter by summer. These changes are part of the natural and harmonious cycle of life. Although at any one time yin or yang may predominate, over time they are in harmony with each other. These changes form part of a complementary cycle, but sometimes yang or yin predominates inappropriately. Excess yang energy results in frenetic activity with no time for rest and renewal; there is excess heat and growth without the cooling effect of yin. Excessive yin results in torpor and sluggishness without the stimulation and fire of yang energy. Landscapes can be classified as representing either yin or yang. A yin landscape is flat, but not totally flat; a yang landscape is mountainous, but not too steep. The extremes would exhibit an excess of that quality. The concept of yin and yang can also be applied to many other situations. The frantic economic activity in many countries during the 1980s can be seen as excessive yang which is, almost inevitably, counterbalanced by a recession, excessive yin. Climates too can be seen as displaying excess yin or yang. A hot dry climate would have excessive yang, whereas a wet cool climate would be showing too much yin. These imbalances within the environment or within a person can lead to physical illness. The particular type of illness is related to whether yin or yang are in excess. Yang illnesses are characterized by heat and activity, yin illnesses by congestion and dampness. Where Ch'i does not flow, paralysis results. Thus, from a Feng Shui point of view, imbalances within an individual will often mirror imbalances within that person's environment. It is also argued that such people would find it difficult, if not impossible, to attain harmony within themselves if there is a lack of harmony in the environment as a result of excessive yin or yang.

It is vitally important therefore that the flow of Ch'i is harmonious: this is seen not as a luxury, but a necessity for happy, healthy and harmonious lives. If Ch'i is already flowing harmoniously, it can often be enhanced to further encourage growth, well-being, abundance and good fortune. Obviously, this has to be done skilfully to ensure that any resulting changes do not result in too much yang energy. An absence of Ch'i, because the flow has been blocked in some way, can lead to barrenness and lack of success. More frequently, Ch'i is flowing, but with an imbalance of yin and yang. If there is too much yin energy, there will be slowness and a lack of vitality, which will need to be counterbalanced by increasing the yang qualities in the landscape. The flow of Ch'i can also exhibit too much yang so that growth is uncontrolled and unbalanced, without attention being paid to nurturing and rest. Here the yin qualities of the landscape would need to be enhanced.

CHOOSING THE SITE

The landscape is first of all assessed and then any buildings sited in the most propitious way, taking into account the natural flow of Ch'i within the landscape and the way in which the landscape will be changed by the construction of the building. If the landscape has a very yang quality, ideally the house would be situated where any yin qualities are present. For example, in a mountainous area, the house would be situated, if possible, in a valley. Preferably the plot on which the building is situated should be square or rectangular, with the building facing south to make maximum use of the sun. The ideal building has a regular shape to it and is often square or rectangular, but because of economic and practical considerations, this is not always possible. Often the Feng Shui expert will have to work with houses which have already been built, rectifying problems arising out of the way in which the building has been sited. This can be a more difficult problem to remedy, especially as practical and economic constraints may limit what can be done. The Feng Shui expert may work on both the house itself and the landscape in which it is situated.

Improving the Landscape

Even if a building cannot be sited in the ideal location, it may be possible to alter the landscape so that Ch'i flows more smoothly and yang and yin achieve some degree of balance. Sometimes the shape of hills and the direction of streams are altered to make the flow of energy healthier. Land may be built up or lowered in order to harmonize the flow of energy. Where the land is very flat, soft hills can be added; where the land is very steep an attempt can be made to round and soften it, reducing abrupt changes of direction. Trees will often be planted in particular places to enhance the correct flow of Ch'i. Water is seen as symbolizing money, because it is essential for the production of rice, so a house with a view of water is much sought after. Businesses also favour a view of water for similar reasons. In Hong Kong it is said that the Hong Kong and Shanghai Bank helped the government with various developments in order to safeguard the view of Victoria Harbour from their building. However, if a building is located on a pointed promontory, there will be nothing to hold the money in. Where a stream runs through a property, this can be auspicious or it can cause money to leave too quickly. A garden pond also needs to be carefully sited: it should be close enough to the building to enhance Ch'i, but not too close to be a potential danger. Stagnant or polluted water may also cause problems for the inhabitants of a building. In geopathic stress terms, water is usually seen as a negative influence on an environment, but this refers to *underground* rather than surface water. Straight roads and rivers are to be avoided as they conduct Ch'i too quickly and have too much yang. A Feng Shui expert would want to change the flow of such a river so that it moved at a slower speed. Otherwise money, health and prosperity would flow through the building rather than be retained within it. Even for those who do not accept the concepts of yin, yang and Ch'i, the recommendations of the Feng Shui expert usually make good sense in practical terms. A very straight river is liable to flood. A house on a flat plain is exposed mercilessly to the elements. Trees correctly planted will protect against harsh winds. A pond or stream too close to a building can undermine the foundations and cause problems with dampness. It is not sensible to live close to polluted water.

Improving the Building

Even if a building is ideally situated in the landscape, the interior of the building can undermine this good fortune and positive flow of Ch'i. But buildings themselves can be modified. The entrance is particularly important, because this is symbolically where Ch'i enters. It needs to be open enough to allow the smooth entry of Ch'i, but enclosed enough to protect the inhabitants. In other words, it needs to embody a balance of yin and yang qualities. The Hong Kong/USA Asian Trade Center in Oakland, California, was altered on the advice of a Feng Shui expert by removing a central column which was said to block the flow of Ch'i at the entrance to the complex. New windows may be put in or corners smoothed. Furniture may be moved into a more pleasing arrangement or may be removed altogether. It is felt that beds and desks should always be placed where it is possible to see the door, partly to avoid being surprised by someone entering unseen.

Mirrors, wind chimes, bells, flutes, mobiles, stones, and statues are used to improve Ch'i within a building. Each type of object has its own characteristic way of influencing Ch'i, and its placing is of vital importance. Several doors aligned in a row are said to encourage Ch'i to move too quickly, so a mobile or wind chime may be hung from one of the door frames to slow this flow. Plants are used to help Ch'i to move more freely and are particularly useful in an area where Ch'i tends to be stagnant. In a dark hallway a Feng Shui expert would consider placing additional lights. Much of the thinking behind using objects to enhance the flow of Ch'i takes into account their symbolic nature. For example, strategically placed bright lights are seen to represent the sun and its positive flow of yang energy, and are used to counter too much dark (yin) energy. Plants remind people of nature and growth. Flutes symbolize safety and good will, because they were used in the past to announce good news. The placing of objects often has a commonsense aspect to it: heavy objects are used to stabilize Ch'i, mirrors are used to reflect negative Ch'i. Sarah Rossbach describes mirrors as 'the all-purpose remedy . . . the aspirin of feng shui'. They can also be used to balance badly proportioned rooms, redirecting Ch'i more positively and counteracting stagnant spots.

Colours are important too, not only in creating a pleasing environment but also for their symbolism: green is used to stimulate growth and yellow to represent the sun. The right object in the wrong place will not do its job effectively and may even damage the flow of Ch'i. In looking at an area it is always important to consider the balance of yin and yang. Adding items with yin qualities to an area with an excess of yin energy will further unbalance the flow of Ch'i and increase the distress of the occupants.

In her book *Interior Design With Feng Shui* (page 123) Sarah Rossbach makes an interesting comment on computers:

> According to modern feng shui experts, computers affect ch'i. Computers can be good, enlivening and stimulating to the office.

They can raise wisdom and knowledge. The computer worker, however, should face the door or he or she will suffer from stress and neurosis after a while.

Feng Shui is concerned with the form and shape of the landscape and buildings and the way in which they mould and distort Ch'i energy. Feng Shui philosophy very firmly locates man in his environment: it is not possible to consider his health without looking at his environment.

Clearly there are a lot of cross-links between geopathic stress and Feng Shui. Both disciplines are concerned with how the environment can influence people. As Nicholas Fernee points out:

> At a more general level the findings of geopathic stress . . . have confirmed the dramatic effect upon health that underground water can have, known in Feng Shui as Sha, or 'noxious vapours', this being an example of negative Chi.[21]

Both GS and Feng Shui are concerned with the energy of places. Both use artifacts – in some cases even the same ones – to alter and improve this energy. Yet whereas the Feng Shui expert, using an Eastern model, speaks of Ch'i and Sha, the person specializing in geopathic stress talks about the electromagnetic spectrum, wave frequencies and resonance.

In spite of all this overlap, this is not to say that correcting geopathic energies automatically corrects Ch'i, or that following Feng Shui precepts will correct all geopathic energies. To some extent the two disciplines are looking at different types of energy, although there is much common ground. It could be argued that for a full appraisal of the energy of a site it would be wise to consult both a Feng Shui expert and someone specializing in geopathic stress. The former would concentrate on bringing harmony and prosperity to the site while the latter would concentrate on correcting the negative earth energies.

9

Self-Help and Protection for the Individual

In Chapter 7 we looked at the various ways of counteracting geopathic stress in buildings; in this chapter we will be looking at how people can protect themselves. Even with their house and work place corrected, people may still encounter geopathic stress when they visit friends, go on holiday, shop, and so on.

Unfortunately one of the problems of being consistently exposed to geopathic stress is that a sufferer's ability to make and carry out decisions becomes undermined. In consequence of this, many people will need help in taking the necessary steps to correct their home or work place and to carry out even the simplest of self-help measures. They frequently seem to lack the energy and determination to change things so that they will no longer be disturbed by these negative energies.

OVERALL HEALTH

An individual's general health will affect his or her ability to resist the effects of geopathic stress. The healthier we are the less susceptible we are to all sorts of geopathic stress. This, of course, applies to any form of stress or toxic overload in our lives. Many people look for a single cause for an illness but, in general, things are much less clear. For most imbalances there will be a number of different factors involved, often building up gradually over time. And it is the sum total of these factors that pushes a person over the threshold into illness. It is not possible to say that one factor is the *cause* of the disease. Although this book focuses on geopathic stress, I am not in any way suggesting that it is *the* cause of illness but rather, it should be seen as a major contributing factor in many health problems. In a way the role of these factors can be likened to a bucket, which fills with a certain amount of water every time one of these factors is present. *Figure 14* represents this visually. If there is severe and long-lasting geopathic stress, a lot of water goes in the bucket. If the exposure is limited, a small amount goes in. Similarly for all the other factors. Symptoms occur when the bucket overflows, but it may have been filling up over a long period of time.

Geopathic stress should be seen as part of the load on an individual. Other factors – including environmental pollution from car exhaust, tobacco smoke and other airborne substances, chemicals in the soil and water, allergies, nutritional deficiencies

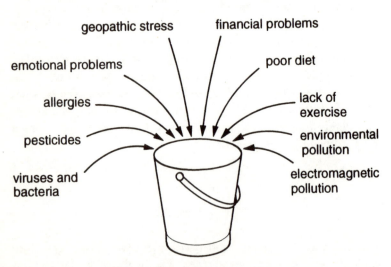

Figure 14 *Stresses which fill 'the bucket'*

and a poor diet, lack of exercise, exposure to viruses and bacteria, electromagnetic pollution from televisions and computers, emotional and financial problems – combine to undermine an individual's health. Intervention in any of these areas can lead to an improvement in health and reduce sensitivity to geopathic stress. As well as tackling geopathic problems, susceptible people should also look to improve their general health in as many ways as possible. However, even if all of these areas are addressed, many individuals will still show a marked sensitivity to negative energies.

FREE RADICALS AND ANTI-OXIDANTS

One very important general health measure is to ensure an adequate intake of anti-oxidants to protect the body against free-radical activity. Professor Gerald Scott of Aston University, a specialist in the understanding of free radicals, told a public enquiry in Yorkshire that power-line electromagnetic fields increase free-radical activity within the body. Free-radical activity is seen as being at least partly responsible for the ageing process and is implicated in degenerative arthritis and cardiovascular disease. Some authorities also feel it is involved in cancer. Free radicals are produced normally as a byproduct of the metabolizing of oxygen and other chemicals in the body. The molecules are highly unstable and seek to combine with other molecules in a destructive manner. The process is similar to what happens when a cut apple becomes brown if left exposed to the air. Anti-oxidants bind with the free radicals, preventing them from attacking cell membranes and tissue linings. For this reason anti-oxidants are often known as free radical scavengers. Vitamin A in the form of beta-carotene, vitamins C and E, the mineral selenium, enzymes such as superoxide dismutase and the amino acid glutathione act as anti-oxidants. There are now many anti-oxidant supplement formulas on the market offering combinations of these nutrients in a single tablet.

REDUCING EXPOSURE TO ELECTROMAGNETIC POLLUTION

It is advisable to reduce the amount of exposure to electromagnetic pollution, particularly while sleeping. This is certainly helpful for many people; some even become quite fanatical about this, removing as many electrical appliances as possible from their homes. This may be necessary in extreme cases, but for most people simple changes can lead to dramatic improvements in health. Many of my clients have found that they sleep better if they either stop using an electric blanket or at least unplug it at the socket at night. Remember, the electric field is still there when the blanket is plugged in but not switched on. Of course, many people have electric clocks and tea-making machines very close to their heads while they sleep and this may be inadvisable for susceptible people. It is very simple to check whether removing these for a time makes any difference to your health in general and to your sleep patterns in particular. Using battery or mechanical clocks in the bedroom is a sensible precaution. Powerwatch UK recommends that electric clocks and tea-making equipment should be kept at least 3 feet from the sleeping position. It has been suggested that metal bed springs can amplify negative energy, so it may be worth considering a mattress of a different construction. Wearing mechanical rather than electronic watches can also make a difference for some people, and reorganizing how computers and word processors are placed in a work environment can have a significant impact on health. Experimenting with some or all of these ideas will quickly show whether or not they are worth persevering with.

If your house is next to an electricity substation it may be as well to organize your sleeping arrangements so that everyone, particularly children, sleep as far away from it as possible. Many scientific authorities do not accept that these substations are a problem, but there is enough concern to make it wise to err on the side of caution.

PROTECTIVE DEVICES

There are many devices now being sold offering protection against geopathic stress and/or electromagnetic pollution. Certainly, almost all of them offer some protection against some forms of geopathic stress, but it is doubtful if any of them, including the ones I recommend personally, protect against *all* forms of it. This does not mean that they are not useful things to have, but it is important that the possession of such a device does not lull the owner into a false sense of security that they are totally protected. Many suppliers will offer a money-back guarantee, allowing the device to be tested with the minimum financial risk.

Owning one of these gadgets is not a substitute for putting a house right. And even if the home and work place is corrected, wearing one of these devices would be an excellent idea for anyone who is particularly susceptible to GS. They are also useful if it is not possible to correct the geopathic problem for some reason, as can happen in some work situations.

Life Transformers

These devices are made by Dr Jimmy Scott, the developer of Health Kinesiology. He has developed a whole series of Life Transformers to help people with a wide variety of problems such as overcoming fears, smoothing the emotions, and improving the memory. Each Life Transformer is a crystal which has been specifically programmed to help the wearer deal with a particular problem, and emits specific energy patterns. Through careful kinesiology testing, Dr Scott found that rose quartz was the best crystal to hold the programme for geopathic stress. It is worn over the upper breast bone and, while not protecting against all forms of GS, does give some real protection against various types of negative energy.

Gizmos

The 'gizmo' helps to correct problems of energy spin. It is about the size of a 10 pence piece and is usually worn on the left side of the body, either directly on the skin or over up to three layers of clothing. Energy spin is affected by exposure to computers, fluorescent lights, televisions, power lines, electronic watches, telephones, microwaves on so on. The 'gizmo', which is made in British Columbia, contains a group of electronic components set in a South African tree resin. The components do not work in the normal electronic manner as there is no battery. In general the device is only worn during waking hours, but occasionally it is worn either all the time or for a few hours a day. The optimum length of time can be established by careful muscle testing or dowsing.

DEGAUSSING THE BODY

One rather bizarre form of treatment which seems to work well for many people is the use of an alternating motor to degauss (demagnetize) the body. The gauss is a unit for measuring the strength of a magnetic field. In individuals who are particularly sensitive to electromagnetic fields, degaussing the body can be helpful. It is also helpful for the many people who are prone to static electric shocks. In fact I would go as far as to say that if you suffer from this, you would definitely benefit from this technique. It is important that an alternating rather than a vibrational motor is used, and probably the most convenient one is that in a hair drier. Once switched on (the exact setting is irrelevant) the hair drier is run over the whole body, with the barrel of the drier against the body. This usually needs to be done on a regular basis. As small babies are sometimes frightened if you attempt to do this to them, it would be better to use a tape head demagnetizer as these are totally silent. The special cassettes that demagnetize tape recorders are *not* suitable. You will need one of the more old-fashioned units that plug in to an electric socket. It is important that you do not have credit cards or other cards with magnetic strips on you while this procedure is being done as there is a possibility that the information encoded on them will be wiped out. This degaussing technique was developed by Dr Jimmy Scott, originator of Health Kinesiology.

The mother of one of my clients commented that she had experienced headaches since going back to work – and only on the days she worked. She was convinced it was because she was working with VDUs, but did not know what to do about it other than give up her job. I suggested she should try using a hair drier in this way once a week for a trial period. Two months later she told me that she had not had a single headache since she started doing this. She was completely mystified as to how this could possibly work, but delighted that she could continue her job without the headaches.

Another client told me his eczema was getting worse again. He had bought a computer and was spending a lot of time using it. Once he started degaussing himself with a hair drier his eczema started to improve again.

A positive but unexpected benefit of degaussing soon became evident. People who spent a lot of time watching television reported that they now found it easier to switch off. They seemed to have lost their 'addiction' to it. This side effect has been so consistent that I now suggest the hair drier technique to anyone who finds they are watching too much television. Here again the benefit will be temporary, so the procedure will need to be repeated on a regular basis.

Even if the house and work space are corrected, some sick people do not regain their former good health. This may be because the geopathic stress has so undermined the body's functioning that treatment needs to be undertaken to strengthen and rebalance it. It is similar to a situation where a fuse blows in an electrical circuit because one too many appliances has been plugged in. Removing the final appliance will not be sufficient to get the system working again: one or more fuses has to be replaced. And to return to the bucket analogy, it is not sufficient to stop putting water in – the bucket has to be emptied. The sick person can do the equivalent of this by consulting a reputable health practitioner, who will work to correct the destruction caused by exposure to geopathic stress. In these cases, practitioners working with subtle energy imbalances seem to achieve better results than those using other therapies.

ADDICTION TO GEOPATHIC STRESS

Complicating matters even further, some people appear to become addicted to geopathic stress in a similar way that people with masked food allergies become addicted to foods. Often their favourite chair will be over the worst point in the house. If they move house, they will often choose one with virtually identical problems. With these people their symptoms have not got worse or suddenly appeared since moving to their present home; they were exposed to the same factors before and their health in all probability has just continued to decline. When the geopathic stress is corrected such people may exhibit a temporary worsening of their symptoms, or even different symptoms. This usually only lasts for a few days. If the problem persists, adjustments may need to be made to the house, perhaps by resiting some of the corrective devices.

At first sight it seems peculiar that we should 'like' things that are bad for us. However, you only have to think about cigarette smoking and drug abuse to know that this occurs regularly. But there are physiological reasons for this. Electromagnetic fields, and so possibly also geopathic stress, can increase the body's production of endorphins, a natural, biological equivalent to morphine. Unfortunately, endorphins, the body's pain killers, are addictive if produced over a long enough period of time. A similar situation may exist when an individual works or lives in an area of high geopathic stress. Consequently, if the situation is corrected and endorphin production stops or is reduced suddenly, the person may feel worse as they are going through a process equivalent to that of drug withdrawal. This in itself is no reason for not dealing with the problems: the reaction to the change in endorphin levels is only temporary in nature and in the long run the affected person is likely to feel much worse if the negative energies are not corrected.

Often it is not enough just to correct a place; if the people living in that environment are to return to full and vibrant health, the damage to those individuals also needs to be addressed. Similarly, it is not enough to help an individual if he or she then goes back to live in the same environment that caused some or all of the damage in the first place. Ideally then, where geopathic stress has undermined a person's health, this two-pronged approach should be implemented.

10

Looking Ahead

Inevitably, some of what has been written in this book is speculative in nature as there is not yet enough evidence to back up our findings. This is partly because of the way scientific research is funded. There is no financial benefit to large companies to prove that electromagnetic fields can cause problems for people. In fact, the opposite could be said to be the case. Much of the research in this area is personally funded by the people doing the work and it may be several years before enough evidence is produced to convince medical and industrial authorities of the need to carry out urgent research. I believe it may be another ten years before there is enough evidence to convince many of the sceptics, but I have no doubt that this will happen. Unfortunately, many of the people working most successfully in this area do not publish (or even publicize) their results. Yet it is vital that this be done, so that an overwhelming body of data can be built up, both in the field of man-made electromagnetic pollution and in the perhaps more difficult area of geopathic stress. Within the former, evidence is mounting regarding exposure to such sources as power lines and VDUs, and this can only help the general understanding and response to the latter.

PREDICTING ILLNESS

The first layer of evidence needed to prove the case for geopathic stress is probably in the area of being able to predict illness based solely on information about a building. Of course, illness can occur even when geopathic stress is not present, so there could not be a total correlation between the two. I personally would like to have the opportunity to look at more offices and factories, so that I can forecast where high levels of absenteeism and sickness are likely to occur. Most critics who dismiss the concept of geopathic stress out of hand are taken aback when they see how it can be used predictively. This is much more convincing than producing evidence showing that people pay me money to fix their houses and then get better. The sceptic will only mutter 'placebo effect' or 'they got better because they paid you'.

Working in an industrial or business setting with geopathic energies in this manner, however, never fails to impress people. They may not immediately accept the idea of geopathic stress, but they accept that I have produced an accurate prediction in a way that they cannot explain. As it would often be possible to correct geopathic problems without employees knowing, subsequent lower absentee and sickness rates would be convincing evidence for many people. This could not be dismissed as a placebo effect if employees were unaware that anything had happened.

EQUIPMENT FOR TESTING

Work is in progress on machines that can detect geopathic energies. If the energies are purely electromagnetic then indeed this may be possible in the not too distant future. There are already some encouraging signs of this, particularly in Germany. However, if some of these negative earth energies are in some way beyond the electromagnetic spectrum this may not be possible in terms of present scientific knowledge. The measurement of at least some of these energies may have to wait for breakthroughs in scientific understanding in other fields.

DOCUMENTATION AND DIFFERENTIATION

For those people who are already convinced of the reality of geopathic stress, there is a need for much more documentation and a clearer description of the individual energies. We must be able to distinguish between them with clarity and accuracy, as it is clear that there are many different types of detrimental earth energies and that they can interact with each other in myriad different ways. In time it may be possible to classify these energies in terms accepted by current scientific understanding (frequency, amplitude, coherence and so on).

In Chapter 6, I mentioned that I am working on a set of homoeopathic potencies of these energies. Dowsers could use these as witnesses, but they will also be available for others in this field to enhance their understanding of the different energies. Many people who hold the vials containing these potentized energies can feel the difference between them. They will sometimes report different sensations within their own body; for example, a tingling in the arm, or a cold feeling in a particular part of the body. Some people feel a difference within the vial itself – it will feel hot or pulsing. Yet other people will experience both a body sensation and a reaction from the vial. Descriptions of these differences will particularly help people who are beginning to work in this field.

Also, more information is needed on precisely how all the materials and devices used for correcting geopathic problems work. Some are clearly linked to fixing particular types of energy, but it seems unlikely that this is true of all of them. Yet there may be some underlying pattern to the various devices that are used for counteracting negative energies. If this is so, an understanding of the connections would be helpful for everyone working in this complex field.

THE LEGAL QUESTION

One interesting development is likely to be in the legal arena. As the concept of geopathic stress and its negative impact on the health of workers becomes more accepted, legal test cases will need to be brought to establish who is responsible for correcting the problems – landlords or tenants. It may well be that this responsibility would have to be written into the lease, in the same way that responsibility for the external maintenance of a building is. Similarly, in new housing developments it would need to be established if it was the builders' responsibility to check for any possible geopathic stress problems both before and during the construction of houses. Such legal cases would obviously increase awareness of the role of geopathic stress in health and well-being. Legislation and regulations seem at the moment a long way off: the existence and effect of negative earth energies have to be established before their legal implications can be considered.

POSITIVE USES OF GEOPATHIC ENERGY

Geopathic stress and electromagnetic pollution are for the most part negative influences on people, but on occasions they can appear to have a benign influence. When I took a friend to an area of high geopathic stress, he said that he really liked it because it made him feel very calm and peaceful. Because he is a man who finds it difficult to relax, he experienced the lowering effect on his energy as calming though this benefit would only be short term. With continuous exposure he too would almost certainly experience ill health and lack of energy.

However, this does suggest a way in which earth energies could be used in the future. It may be possible to manipulate the energies of individual rooms to provide either calm and relaxing places for sleep and rest, or more stimulating environments for work. This would take into account the Feng Shui concepts of yin and yang. A bedroom would require more yin characteristics, whereas an office space would probably need more yang. Each room would have a thermostat so that its energy could be adjusted, in the same way as temperature and lighting are today.

Electromagnetic waves are also being harnessed in the cause of healing. On a visit to Russia, Dr Cyril Smith saw millimetre microwaves being used to treat pain in the hand. He is quoted as saying:

> All in all, I saw concern for the environmental health aspects of EMFs as well as wide spread applications of the therapeutic uses of EMFs in the USSR . . . They ranged from the diagnostic applications covering the whole of the electromagnetic spectrum to the electrical stimulation of bone healing and the application of millimetre wavelengths for therapeutic purposes.[22]

TOWARDS A MORE HOLISTIC MODEL

Geopathic energies challenge our current understanding of how bodies work and what affects them. Incorporating our knowledge of these phenomena into our understanding of illness requires a much more holistic view of man: one which takes into account the role of Ch'i, the subtle bodies, the meridians, the chakras and yin and yang. This view of man sees the importance of harmony and balance, both within the body and between people and their environment.

Tom Graves, in his book *Needles of Stone Revisited*, sees the ancient standing stones as part of the healing of the earth, in some way akin to a form of acupuncture for the earth. Some of the energy lines traversing the earth can be seen as part of the earth's own etheric body. These ideas lead on to the idea of the earth having its own subtle energy system and its own homoeostatic health-maintaining mechanisms.

In *Gaia, The Practical Science of Planetary Medicine* (page 11) James Lovelock sees the earth as:

> a single physiological system, an entity that is alive at least to the extent that, like other living organisms, its chemistry and temperature are self-regulating at a state favourable for life.

He calls for the development of a planetary medicine that would be concerned with the health of the earth. Amongst many other issues, he argues for the protection of the forests and attention to the problems of pollution. I would like to add to this a concern with geopathic stress energies and Feng Shui principles so that a state favourable for life can be maintained.

Michael Shallis in *The Electric Shock Book* (page 263) remarks:

> Electricity and magnetism can be seen as the intermediary between the material world and the ethereal world, touching us physically but also linking us to other realms of the totality of creation. It is through electromagnetism that we can perceive the subtle forces that operate in those intangible regions.

Above all, these unseen energies help to remind us that we too are more than just physical bodies with a mind, that we too have dimensions beyond what our normal senses can understand. We have an energy presence that can be disturbed by other energy presences, and we ignore this fact at our peril.

The idea that petrol and diesel exhaust fumes, pesticides, artificial colours and additives could contribute to ill health was once regarded as a bizarre notion. Now it is part of mainstream thinking and understanding. This will also be the experience of geopathic stress. Continuous or repeated exposure to GS will come to be seen as a major contributing factor to a whole range of illnesses, and it will be recognized that it is essential to consider this possibility in all illnesses. In order to be able to treat these matters seriously, medical doctors and alternative practitioners will need to have an understanding of this phenomenon. This book is a contribution to bringing that day closer.

APPENDIX:
Sick Building Syndrome

In Chapter 1 we saw how geopathic stress is often one of the factors involved in sick building syndrome. This is a relatively new phenomenon and the wider issues it raises merit a little more discussion. Sick building syndrome is said to occur when a large number of people complain of symptoms of ill health which coincide with their being in a particular building. Most of the interest in this area has stemmed from problems with offices, although it is not confined solely to this type of environment. The World Health Organization defines sick building syndrome as 'a syndrome of complaints covering non-specific feelings of malaise the onset of which is associated with occupancy of certain buildings'.

In 1987 Wilson and Hedge[23] surveyed 4,373 people working in 46 buildings and found that 80 per cent had symptoms which they attributed to the building they worked in. Sceptics argue that people bring these illnesses and dissatisfaction to work with them and then because they spend so much of their waking time working (often at jobs which they do not enjoy) they blame these on the building where they work. Even when many people in an office are complaining of feeling unwell this is put down to hysteria. The fact that symptoms may clear or lessen during holiday periods does not convince the sceptics either, as they argue that the person's symptoms have improved simply because they are not working. However, as more work has been done in this area and measurable results have been shown, the number of sceptics has diminished.

Sick building syndrome is usually defined in terms of inadequate ventilation and heating, chemical contamination (from photocopiers, carpets etc) and problems related to moulds and bacteria. Complaints about sick buildings fall into two categories: the building is causing illness or is causing discomfort. Illnesses commonly reported include tiredness, confusion, headaches, flu-like symptoms, skin rashes, problems with the eyes, nose, throat and chest (often involving a feeling of dryness in the mucous membranes), dizziness and nausea. These symptoms will result in absenteeism, increased staff turnover, reduced efficiency and lowered morale.

The problem is thought to have arisen as a direct result of the development of engineering technology, as many buildings are effectively sealed by their air conditioning and security systems. Several decades ago employees could open and close windows in individual offices, adjust lighting to suit their own needs, increase or decrease privacy by opening or closing doors. Now people frequently work in large open-plan offices where the heating, ventilation and lighting are controlled centrally for large areas that affect many people. Windows are not designed to open because this undermines the efficiency of the heating system. In addition, it is cheaper to re-circulate air than to bring in a constant supply of air from outside. Increased security means that many doors are kept closed. Consequently, employees often feel powerless to change their environment. The old working environments were often far from comfortable, but people at least felt that they had some ability to change the situation. Often the owners of the building will blame the architects and engineers for not putting in adequate systems, and the engineers and architects in their turn will blame the owner of the building for not maintaining the infrastructure adequately.

McIntyre and Sterling[24] identified six factors that were consistently linked with suggestions of sick building syndrome. These are:

- a sealed building where windows cannot be opened at will
- a mechanical heating and ventilation system

- use of equipment giving off fumes (eg photocopiers)
- fluorescent lighting
- concern with energy conservation
- lack of individual control over the working environment

Dr Surrinder Johal in a report produced by the UK Laboratory of the Government Chemist also adds that clerical staff are more likely to suffer than managerial staff and that the people with the most symptoms are indeed those who least feel that they have control over their environment.

Even in the best managed working environments it is impossible to set the temperature, lighting and humidity at levels which are acceptable to everyone. However, the UK Chartered Institution for Building Services Engineers has produced recommendations to control the various factors implicated in sick building syndrome[25]:

Temperature	19–23°C
Relative humidity	40–70% (at least 55% where underfloor heating is installed)
Fresh air	8 litres (488 cubic inches) per second per person minimum
	25 litres (1,526 cubic inches) per second in areas of heavy smoking
Total air supply	4–6 air changes per hour
Air speed	0.1–0.3 metres (4–12 inches) per second

The different factors (temperature, humidity and air movement) interact. For example, if humidity is low then it will appear cooler than if humidity is high. The above figures suggest that ideal conditions can be assessed relatively easily, but at best it is a compromise between individual preferences and the economic and practical considerations of the site. Different people prefer different conditions: the same person may even require different conditions at different times of the day. This individuality is particularly true for people suffering from an illness. Some asthmatics, for example, find their asthma is better for dry heat whereas others would prefer a more humid environment. It is widely recognized that even when a building has been designed and built to the best standards and the infrastructure is properly maintained, some people will still be dissatisfied with it, because of individual preferences which are far from the norm. Many buildings are not built to the most exacting standards, partly because this is very expensive, so judgements have to be made as to what is acceptable. While it is important for fresh air to be brought in, for instance, sometimes this may be more contaminated than air which has been circulating within the building for some time. In this case a decision has to be made: is it better to re-circulate the air or to have the extra cost of cleaning up the fresh air? Plant rooms housing air conditioning equipment and the ducts and piping that carry heat and air around the building are usually required to be kept to a minimum as these reduce the amount of leasable space. If the ducts are too small, however, the air conditioning and heating system will be inadequate.

Problems attributed to sick building syndrome often dissipate when ventilation is improved. However, it is unclear whether faulty or inadequate ventilation is the cause of the problem. It is possible that by improving ventilation other agents such as moulds, cigarette smoke and chemicals are lessened, and that it is this reduction rather than the increase in ventilation itself which leads to the improvement.

There have been many changes in building materials over the last few decades with synthetics replacing natural materials. Some of these newer materials give off gases, which are known to be toxic in large quantities. The number of chemicals involved is large and some of them are known carcinogens. The list includes formaldehyde, benzene and hydrocarbons.

- *Formaldehyde* is one of the most common chemicals in the environment. For instance, it is found in glues, foam upholstery and various plastics. It is a highly toxic substance; in addition, many people seem to be allergic to it, showing reactions even when their exposure is significantly below levels which are regarded as toxic by the experts.
- *Benzene* is found in tobacco smoke, some plastics and cleaning solutions.
- *Hydrocarbons* are found in paint, synthetic materials, floor and furniture polishes and vehicle fumes.

When buildings are new, people are aware of the chemicals in the atmosphere, but as a building becomes older and their concentration in the air drops, they become less obvious. While higher levels are likely to cause more problems, even relatively low levels of some of these contaminants are now being shown to be harmful to susceptible people.

The list of culprits also includes natural substances. Where heating and ventilation systems are inadequately maintained these then provide an ideal environment for the proliferation of airborne bacteria and moulds, such as *aspergillus alternaria*, *cladosporium* and *stemphylium*. Humidifiers in particular are often responsible for problems in this area. For many people the constant day by day exposure to high levels of mould spores can lead to respiratory problems and a general feeling of being unwell. In a well-managed building the incidence of moulds will certainly be less than in many houses, but regular maintenance of the unseen infrastructure of a building is sometimes neglected, allowing the moulds to grow. Often employees are not aware of these natural and chemical airborne contaminants, so they do not understand the cause of their ill health.

For a full understanding of the effect of buildings on their occupants it is always necessary to look at the problem of geopathic stress. Indeed many of the professionals involved in looking after buildings and their occupants will readily admit that even when the air conditioning and office environment have been optimized there can still be apparently intractable problems of dissatisfaction and illness among the occupants of the building. Some of these can be explained in terms of individual preferences and some are undoubtedly expressions of an underlying dissatisfaction with the job. Yet often even when these factors are taken into account, a core of ill health among the building's occupants remains unaccounted for. In this situation an appraisal of geopathic stress would be advisable.

NOTES

1. Christopher Bird, *The Divining Hand*, pp 270-2 (see Bibliography for details)
2. *Here's Health*, October 1991
3. *Caduceus*, No 7, 1989
4. Christopher Bird, *The Divining Hand*, p 276 (see Bibliography for details)
5. Christopher Bird, *The Divining Hand*, p 269 (see Bibliography for details)
6. Christopher Bird, *The Divining Hand*, p 270 (see Bibliography for details)
7. *Electromagnetic Fields and the Risk of Cancer*, p 130 (see Bibliography for details)
8. Nancy Wertheimer and Ed Leeper, *American Journal of Epidemiology*, Vol 109, 1979
9. *Sick Building Syndrome*, pp 75 and 63 (see Bibliography for details)
10. *What Doctors Don't Tell You*, Vol 3, No 6
11. *What Doctors Don't Tell You*, Vol 3, No 7
12. Report in *The Guardian*, 15 July 1994
13. *International Industrial Biotechnology Journal*, April 1986
14. *International Industrial Biotechnology Journal*, April 1986
15. *International Journal of Alternative and Complementary Medicine*, January 1993
16. *International Journal of Alternative and Complementary Medicine*, July 1992
17. *International Journal of Alternative and Complementary Medicine*, May 1994
18. *Catalyst*, No 13, 1993

19 *International Journal of Alternative and Complementary Medicine*, January 1994
20 Foreword to David Tansley, *Radionics Interface with the Ether Fields*
21 'Wind and Water', *International Journal of Alternative and Complementary Medicine*, August 1993
22 Article on EMFs in *Journal of Alternative Medicine*, November 1989
23 Wilson S and Hedge A, *The Office Environment Survey: A Study of Building Sickness*, Building Use Studies, 53–54 Newman Street, London W1P 3PG, UK, Tel: 0171 580 8848
24 McIntyre E D and Sterling E M, *Building Environment Modification: An Experimental Study*. Paper presented at the Indoor Air Conference, Seattle, 7–9 December 1982
25 CIBSE Guide A: Design Data, 1986

BIBLIOGRAPHY

Bachler, Kathe, *Earth Radiation*, Wordmasters Ltd, 1989
Beijns, Charles, *A New Energetic Technology*, a booklet available from Herbamin describing the Apopi spheres
Bird, Christopher, *The Divining Hand*, Whitford Press, 1993
Brennan, Barbara Ann, *Hands of Light*, Bantam, 1988
Chopra, Deepak, *Quantum Healing*, Bantam, 1990
Choy, Ray V S, Monroe, Jean A and Smith, Cyril W 'Electrical Sensitivity in Allergy Patients', *Clinical Ecology*, Vol IV, No 3, 1986
Coghill, Roger, 'Discovering Light in the Darkness', *International Journal of Alternative and Complementary Medicine*, September 1989
Davidson, John, *Radiation*, C W Daniel Co Ltd, 1986
Devereux, Paul, *Places of Power*, Blandford, 1990
Eabry, Steve, 'Biogenic Magnetite in Humans', *International Journal of Alternative and Complementary Medicine*, January 1993
Electromagnetic Fields and the Risk of Cancer, National Radiological Protection Board, Chilton, Didcot, Oxon, OX11 0RQ
Fernee, Nicholas, 'Wind and Water: a Brief Introduction to Feng Shui', *International Journal of Alternative and Complementary Medicine*, August 1993
Gerber, Richard, *Vibrational Medicine*, Bear & Company Publishing, 1988
Graves, Tom, *The Dowser's Workbook*, The Aquarian Press, 1989
Graves, Tom, *Needles of Stone Revisited*, Gothic Image Publications, 1978
Havelock Fidler, J, *Ley Lines*, Turnstone Press Ltd, 1983
Gordon, Rolf, *Are You Sleeping in a Safe Place?*, Dulwich Health Society, 130 Gipsy Hill, London SE19 1PL

Graves, Tom and Hoult Janet (ed), *The Essential T.C. Lethbridge*, Routledge & Kegan Paul, 1980

Heselton, Philip, *The Elements of Earth Mysteries*, Element Books Ltd, 1991

Kenyon, Julian, 'Bio-energetic Regulatory Medicine', *International Journal of Alternative and Complementary Medicine*, January 1994

Lovelock, James, *Gaia: The Practical Science of Planetary Medicine*, Gaia Books Ltd, 1991

Martin, Simon, 'Every Illness Has Its Place', *Here's Health*, October 1991

Philpott, William, 'Biomagnetics: the value of using negative magnetic energy in diabetes mellitus', *International Journal of Alternative and Complementary Medicine*, July 1992

Philips, Alasdair, *Living With Electricity*, Powerwatch UK, c/o 2 Tower Road, Sutton, Ely, Cambs, CB6 2QA

Rossbach, Sarah, *Feng Shui*, Rider, 1992

Rossbach, Sarah, *Interior Design with Feng Shui*, Rider, 1991

Schmidt, Paul, *Earth Rays*, Rayonex GmbH, Postfach 4060, D-5940 Lennestadt 14, Germany

Shallis, Michael, *The Electric Shock Book*, Souvenir Press, 1988

Sheldrake, Rupert, *A New Science of Life*, Paladin, 1987

Sick Building Syndrome, London Hazards Centre, Headland House, 308 Gray's Inn Road, London WC1X 8DS, 1990

Smith, Cyril, 'High-Sensitivity Biosensors and Weak Environment Stimuli', *International Industrial Biotechnology*, April/May 1986

Smith, Cyril W and Best, Simon, *Electromagnetic Man*, J M Dent & Sons Ltd, 1988

Spangler, David, 'Making The Energies Work For You', *Catalyst*, No 13, 1993

Tansley, David V, *Radionics Interface With the Ether Fields*, C W Daniel Co Ltd, 1986

Thurnell-Read, Jane, 'Geopathic Stress', *International Journal of Alternative and Complementary Medicine*, April 1994

Thurnell-Read, Jane, *Health Kinesiology: The Muscle Testing System That Talks To The Body*, Life-Work Potential, 2002

Turner, Ronnie, 'The Lecher Antenna: New Insights into the Human Energy Fields', *International Journal of Alternative and Complementary Medicine*, May 1994

USEFUL ADDRESSES

Australia

Australian Kinesiology Association
PO Box 233,
Kerrimuir, VIC 3129
www.aka-oz.org

Feng Shui Society of Australia
PO Box 597
Epping, NSW 2121

Canada

Canadian Association of Specialized Kinesiology Association (CANASK)
Apt 321, 1333 Hornby Street,
Vancouver, BC, V6Z 2C1
Tel: 669 8481 Fax: 669 8099
Email: canask@vcn.bc.ca

Canadian Society of Dowsers
1011 Upper Middle Rd. E. Suite 1219,
Oakville, ON, L6H 5Z9
Tel: 888 588 8958
www.canadiandowsers.org

Efstonscience, Inc
3350 Dufferin Street
Toronto, ON, MBA 3A4
www.e-sci.com
Tel: 416 787 4581
(For magnets etc.)

Jimmy Scott
Birdsalls House
RR3
Hastings, ON, K0L 1Y0
Tel: 705 696 3176
Fax: 705 696 3664
(For gizmos and geopathic stress Life Transformers. Also for information on Health Kinesiology practitioners and Health Kinesiology training courses.)

Europe

Belgium

Arophar
Papenboskant 85
B-1861 Meise
Tel: 052 30 39 36
(The manufacturer of Apopi spheres.)

Editions Sevranx
23/25 Rue Gustave Biot
B-1050 Bruxelles
Tel: 02649 1840
Fax: 02649 1210
(The makers of Cosmic Batteries.)

New Zealand

Touch for Health Kinesiology Association of New Zealand (Inc.)
www.tfhkinesiologynz.mybravenet.com/tfh.htm

UK

Eddie Borrelli
69 Drift Way,
Cirencester,
Gloucestershire GL7 1WN
Tel: 01285 641979
(Copper coils for use in correcting geopathic stress available by post.)

Useful Addresses

The British Society of Dowsers
Sycamore Barn
Hastingleigh,
Ashford,
Kent TN25 5HW
Tel: 01233 750253
www.britishdowsers.org
(The society offers public lectures and short courses on dowsing. It also has a comprehensive list of books available for purchase.)

The Chartered Institution of Building Services Engineers
Delta House
222 Balham High Road,
London SW12 9BS
Tel: 020 8675 5211
Fax: 020 8675 5449
www.cibse.org

Dulwich Health
130 Gipsy Hill,
London SE19 1PL
Tel/Fax: 020 8670 5883
www.dulwichhealth.co.uk
(Information on and products for geopathic stress, magnetic therapy and sick building syndrome.)

The Feng Shui Society
377 Edgware Road,
London W2 1BT
Tel: 07050 289 200

Health Kinesiology UK
Silver Birches, 44 Woodland Way,
Old Tupton, Chesterfield,
Derbyshire S42 6JA
Tel: 08707 655980 (for UK HK practitioners)
Tel: 01246 862339 (for UK HK training)
Email: hk4health@hotmail.com
www.hk4health.com
(For training courses and practitioners of Health Kinesiology in the UK.)

Herbamin
PO Box 5,
Albury,
Surrey GU5 9DN
Tel: 01483 202047
(The UK importer of Apopi spheres.)

Kinesiology Federation
PO Box 17153,
Edinburgh EH11 3WQ
Tel/Fax: 08700 113545
Email: kfadmin@kinesiologyfederation.org
www.kinesiologyfederation.org

MMG MagDev Ltd
Unit 17,
Highworth Industrial Park
Highworth,
Swindon,
Wiltshire SN6 7NA
Tel: 01793 766001
Fax: 01793 765576
www.magdev.co.uk
(A source of suitable magnets for GS work.)

Stella Martin
19 The Broadway,
Chichester,
West Sussex PO19 6QR
Tel: 01243 781379
(For Health Through The Eyes symbols.)

Powerwatch UK
www.powerwatch.org.uk
(Formed in 1989 to oppose the building of a large electricity substation. Now co-ordinates a strategic approach to EMF hazards nationwide. They hire out hand-held meters for measuring electric and magnetic fields in your home or work place.)

Useful Addresses

Jane Thurnell-Read
Sea View House,
Long Rock, Penzance,
Cornwall TR20 8JF
Tel: 01736 719030
Fax: 01736 719040
Email: jane@lifeworkpotential.com
www.lifeworkpotential.com
(Geopathic stress consultations undertaken. For purchase of Life Transformers.)

What Doctors Don't Tell You PLC
2 Salisbury Road,
London SW19 4EZ
Tel: 0870 4449886
www.wddty.co.uk
(Produces a newsletter of the same name that regularly includes articles on electromagnetic pollution.)

Wholistic Research Company Limited
Unit 1, Enterprise Park,
Claggy Road, Kimpton,
Hertfordshire SG4 8HP
Tel: 01438 833100 Fax: 01438 833541

USA

American Society of Dowsers,
Box 24,
Danville, VT 05828

Essentia Communications
1572 Eton Way,
Crofton, MD 21114
Tel: 410 721 8522
Fax: 410 721 5122
E-mail: kim@essentiaco.com
www.essentiaco.com

INDEX

absorption of energies 77, 79
acupuncture 52–3, 57, 69
alarm reaction 37
allergies 22, 25, 39, 82, 100, 106
aluminium 78, 82–3
animals 10–11, 63
anti-oxidants 101
Apopi spheres 85
Applied Kinesiology 69
arthritis 69, 101
astral body *see* emotional body
atoms 49

Bachler, Kathe 43, 76
Beijns, Charles 85
Best, Simon 23
beta particles 39
Bird, Christopher 43, 64, 67
birth defects 13, 22, 24
black lines 29
black water 27
blocking of energies 77–8
blood polarity 45
body polarity 45
brain rhythms 40
Brennan, Barbara Ann 60
Brewer, James 25
British Society of Dowsers 68

cancer xii, 13, 21, 22, 24, 25, 28, 45, 56, 101
cardiovascular disease 101
cats 9, 11, 63
cellular renewal 40–1
ceremonies 89
chakras 39, 47, 55–7, 89, 112
Ch'i 51–3, 57, 60, 91, 92, 94–8, 112
Chopra, Deepak 41

Choy, V S 25
classrooms 101
Clinical Kinesiology 69
Coghill, Roger 24
coils 80
colour 84, 97
computers 23–4, 47
copper 78, 83
cosmic batteries 83
cosmic rays 5, 28
cows 12
crystals 79–80, 103
Curry, Manfred 27–8
Curry lines 27–8, 29

Davidson, John 42, 49–50
degaussing 104–5
depression 22
Devereux, Paul 46
diabetes 45
dogs 11, 63
Douglas, Herbert 43
dowsing 26, 29, 64, 65–8, 72, 78, 79, 82, 88, 110
Dulwich Health Society x–xi, 2
dyslexia 69

Eabry, Steve 24, 44
earache 82
earthquake 2
eczema 69, 105
elder 78
electrical activity in the body 39–40
electrical fields 17–18, 19, 43, 102, 104, 108
electromagnetic fields (EMFS) 19, 21–5, 40, 101, 106, 112

128

Index

electromagnetic pollution 1, 17, 18–25, 26, 47, 101, 102, 108, 111
electromagnetic smog *see* electromagnetic pollution
electromagnetic spectrum 14–18, 47, 48, 78, 98, 109
elm 78
emotional body 53
emotionally charged stones 35
emotional problems 24, 101
endorphins 106
energy 50
energy clouds 30, 74
energy drains 31–2, 74, 89
energy lines 9, 43, 74, 112
energy spin 104
environmental pollution 100
etheric body 39, 41, 47, 51, 53, 56–7, 112
exercise 100–1
extremely low frequency waves (ELFs) 20
eye problems 8, 23

faith healing 57
Feng Shui 91–2, 94–8, 111, 113
Fernee, Nicholas 98
financial problems 101
flutes 97
foundations 3, 4
free radicals 100

gamma rays 3, 17, 39, 78
General Adaption Syndrome (GAS) 37
geological faults 2
geopathic energy, and other subtle energies 48
 sensitivity to 46
 sources 1–5
geopathic stress, addiction to 106–7
 definition ix
 effects 5–13, 34–37
 symptoms 5, 8, 10, 13, 106
Gerber, Richard 45, 51, 53, 79
Girdlestone, Rodney 3
gizmos 104
Goodheart, George 68–9
Gordon, Rolf x–xi, 2–3
Grafenau xii
graphite 78
Graves, Tom 33, 68, 112

Hartmann, Ernst 28
Hartmann lines 28–9
Harvalik, Zaboj V 67–8

Havelock Fidler, J 33, 89
headaches 8, 13, 22, 82, 105
healthcare xiii
Health Kinesiology xiii, 32, 69, 70, 71, 82
Health Through The Eyes 88
homoeopathy 46, 57
homoeostatic mechanism 71, 112
Hong Kong and Shanghai Bank 95
Hong Kong/USA Asian Trade Center 96
horses 11–12
hospitals 9–10
houses 11–12
Hyde Park 64
hyperactivity 13

infertility 13
inflammation 28
insomnia 22
Institute of Noetic Studies 58–9
iron 78, 83
irritability 20, 22

Kenyon, Julian 51
kinesiology 26, 29, 31, 57, 64, 68–72, 78, 79, 81, 82, 84, 88, 103
Kirlian, Semyon 49
Kirlian photography 49
Kopp, Joseph 11, 12

landscape 94–6, 98
Lethbridge, T C 31, 67, 78, 89
leukaemia 20, 25
ley lines 1, 32–3, 77
Life Transformers 103
light 15
London Hazards Centre 23
Lovelock, James 112
lymphoma 25

magnetic fields 1–4, 14, 17–18, 19, 43
magnetism 44–6
magnetite 44
magnets 84–5
ME 113, 25
Melzer xiii
memory 69
mental body 53
meridians 39, 50–3, 57, 70, 88, 112
metal plates 83
microwaves 15, 17, 20, 49, 112
migraine 23, 69

mining 3, 4
mirrors 78, 80–2, 97
miscarriage 13, 23
mobiles 97
molecules 49, 101
morphic resonance 60–1
moulds 12–13
muscles 68–71

Naccachian, René 45
nanoteslas 22
NASA 31, 86
nausea 20
National Radiological Protection Board 21
nose problems 8
Nottingham 59
NUTEK 22
nutrition 100–1

offices 7– 9, 114–18
ore masses 2

paranormal phenomena 34–5
Philpott, William 44–5
photographs 86
physical body 51, 53, 54, 56–7, 58
plants 11–12, 63–4, 86, 97
Pohl, Gustav von xii
power lines 1, 20, 22, 47, 84, 108
Powerwatch UK 23, 102
psoriasis 15
psychic detection of energies 72–3

quartz 78, 79

radiation, ionizing 20, 22, 23
radio waves 1, 15, 17, 20
reflection of energies 77, 78, 80
resistance reaction 37
resonance 41–3, 98
Rivett, Peter 40
roads 10
rods 83–4
Rossbach, Sarah 91, 92, 97–8

Schmidt, Paul 5
Schumann, W O 31
Schumann waves 31
Scott, Gerald 101
Scott, Jimmy 32, 103, 105
Seasonal Affective Disorder (SAD) 15
Selye, Hans 37

Sha 98
Shallis 112
shapes 86
Sheldrake, Rupert 58–9
shops 7
sick building syndrome 8–9, 114–18
Silk, Anne 23
skin problems 8, 15
sleep problems 13
Smith, C W 39, 43, 111
Spangler, David 50
spirals 30, 74
spiritual body 53, 54
spots 30
Stängle, Jacob 3
steel 78, 83
stomach problems 81–2
stress 36–8, 69
Stuttgart xii
subtle bodies 53–7, 59, 112
subtle energy 48–50, 57–8, 106
subtle energy systems 38–9, 47, 50–1, 58, 112
symbols 86–9

Tansley, David 60
Tacoma bridge 42
television waves 17, 20, 21
Thames Water Ring Main 3–4
tiredness 8
Turner, Ronnie 45

underground transport systems 3
utilities 3, 4

Vilsbiburg xii
visual display units (VDUs) 23–4, 104, 108

water 1, 2, 27, 77, 78, 91, 95–6
waves 15–17, 20, 84, 98
Westlake, Aubrey 64
Willings, Heather 88
wind 91, 96
wind chimes 97
Winzer xii
Wittmann, Dr 27

x-rays 17, 78

yin and yang 92–4, 97, 111, 112